# OVER THE FRONT

# OVER THE FRONT

A Complete Record of
the Fighter Aces and Units
of the United States and
French Air Services,
1914-1918

Norman L.R.Franks & Frank W.Bailey

GRUB STREET · LONDON

Published by
Grub Street
The Basement
10 Chivalry Road
London SW11 1HT

Copyright © 1992 Grub Street, London
Text copyright © 1992 Norman Franks and Frank Bailey

Maps by Robert Franks

British Library Cataloguing in Publication Data

Franks, Norman L. R.
    Over the Front: Complete Record of the
    Fighter Aces and Units of the United
    States and French Air Services, 1914-18
    I. Title   II. Bailey, Frank W.
    940.4

    ISBN 0-948817-54-2

Typeset by BMD Graphics, Hemel Hempstead

Printed and bound by Biddles Ltd, Guildford and King's Lynn

# Acknowledgements

The authors wish to acknowledge and thank the following people and organisations for their
assistance over a period of years, which has enabled them to amass the information necessary to
make this book possible.

The Bureau Central d'Incorporation et d'Achives, de l'Armee de l'Air and the Service Historique
de l'Armee de l'Air (SHAA), provided much information relative to French escadrille histories and
personal biographies. The British Public Records Office, Kew, Surrey, England. The US National
Archives

The following persons also contributed information, photos and other material which added to the
authenticity of the victory lists and biographies;

Chaz Bowyer, George H Williams, A E Clausen Jr., Peter Kilduff, Mike O'Neil, Richard Duiven,
Dr James Davilla, Jack Eder, Jon Guttman, Neal O'Conner, Nick Mladenoff, August G Blume,
John Linneman, Daniel Brunet, Daniel Porret, and not forgetting the late O A Sater, Dennis
Connell, Paul Joli, Dr Gustav Bock, Steve St. Martin, Paul Chamberlain and Russ Manning.

Also thanks to Robert Franks for producing the two maps.

# Contents

## AUTHORS' NOTE

For the sake of ease and clarity, no accents appear on any of the French words in the book. The reader will also detect a variation in spelling between Adjudant and Adjutant. It is the same rank. Finally, every care has been taken with spelling of names and place names. However, because the research was often taken from old, sometimes faulty, records, some mis-spellings may appear. It is hoped they have been kept to a minimum.

# Introduction

This is a companion volume to Grub Street's *Above the Trenches* by Christopher Shores, Norman Franks and Russell Guest, published in 1990. It will be followed by a third volume concerning the German aces of WWI. These volumes, apart from producing a record and mini-biography of all pilots termed as 'aces' by the general public, and some air forces in particular, also show how an individual pilot's victory score was made up, with dates and enemy types, etc, rather than just to acknowledge an arbitrary victory total.

As with the earlier book, some clarification of victory claims by both the American and French Air Forces in WWI is necessary. And there are basic differences in how the Americans and French gave official credit for air combat claims, to the way the British, Royal Flying Corps, Royal Naval Air Service and Royal Air Force gave credits.

The British decided early in the war to give credits for what may be termed 'probable' victories, due to the fact that the vast majority of the air war was fought over the German side of the front line trenches and confirmation in the form of wreckage, prisoners, etc, was more difficult. Provided, therefore, that a competent witness saw and confirmed seeing an aeroplane going down "out of control" — in a way which seemed highly likely that it would eventually crash, then the victorious pilot would be given credit for an 'out of control' victory. Thus a pilot with say, 10 victories, might have this broken down, in reality, to 'seven destroyed and three out of control'. For further explanations of the British scoring system, the reader is directed to read the introduction to the first volume.

The French Air Service instigated a different method of assigning credits for air victories. They had to be seen and confirmed by independent observers – another pilot, a ground soldier or artillery man, and so on — to actually be destroyed. That is to say, it had to be seen to fall in flames, fall and crash into the ground, disintegrate in the air, or be forced to land 'inside' Allied lines and be captured. Probable victories, where they were seen to spin down out of control but their final end not observed, or if a crash or burning was seen but was not corroborated by at least one other person, while it would be noted and possibly agreed a probable victory, would not be added to a pilot's personal victory score.

As many American pilots flew with the French in the early years of the war, and others joined the Lafayette Escadrille and then the Lafayette Flying Corps, it was natural for these American pilots to have exactly the same rules apply to them. Therefore, when the new United States Air Service began to arrive in France in late 1917, the General HQ, American Expeditionary Force, adopted the same French rules for its own Air Service victory credits. Therefore, American pilots and air gunner/observers were only credited with 'confirmed' victories that were actually seen to be destroyed, but not probable victories. Not even those seen to land in enemy occupied territory, whether they supposed the pilot and or pilot and gunner had been seriously wounded or even killed. If the aeroplane seemed intact, then there was no accredited victory. As Maxwell AFB confirmed: "The fact that an enemy aircraft was 'out of control', even if a result of combat, was not sufficient for official confirmation of a victory. Not only did the aircraft have to impact the ground and be destroyed or captured, the destruction had to be witnessed and confirmed by a 'competent witness', or the wreckage found at the location specified by the pilot. The pilot could not confirm his own claim, nor could any crew member of his aircraft."

The only difference in this respect was for the Americans who flew with the 17th and 148th Aero Squadrons, under British Control in the summer of 1918. They were given 'out of control' victories in their scores because that is how the British system worked. This applied equally to American pilots who served entirely with other RFC, RNAS or RAF units. Therefore, in the ace biographies which follow, those American pilots given credit for 'out of control' victories in their final scores are shown here too. In these particular cases, the final category is shown by each entry, eg: DES, OOC.

Contrary to popular belief, and certainly discovered beyond doubt in research for *Above the Trenches*, shared victories were awarded when two or more pilots had a hand in the destruction of one enemy plane. On occasions there could be up to seven or eight pilots given a share in one victory. Thus, for instance, the total credits shown in the American Air Force's Study 133, total 1,513, for the overall destruction of 756 German airplanes and 76 kite balloons.

No fewer than 341 victories were shared to some degree. We are not making any point in saying this, merely recording a fact for general clarification.

Notes on the confirmation sources can vary, but they are given where known. For the British, this could be merely because a combat report had been filled out and 'agreed' by Wing HQ, and/or it appeared in the RFC/RNAS/RAF communiques, which in any event were only noted as a matter of interest and not, as many suppose, an official acknowledgement of a victory! The American pilots had their confirmations generally reported in French Communiques – which were an official acknowledgement, or in General Orders, also an official acknowledgement. Occasional references to Wing or Squadron records, (WD, SR, V Bde, or a Public Record Office Air 1 reference number) indicate a source of verification of a claim having been submitted. With the French confirmation, the sources are usually from the communiques but other references may come from the Resume Operations Aerienne, Group d'Armee Reserve (GAR), Division d'Armee Aerienne, (DAR), Compt Rendu (CR), Groupe de Combat records (GC), or specific Army records, eg: IVe (4th Armee Rendu) or Ve (5th Armee Rendu).

Reference too, to US133, indicates that US credits were acknowledged in the US Air Service Victory Credits, World War I, produced by the Historical Research Division, at Maxwell Air Force Base, Alabama in June 1969. However, it should be noted that there are just a few errors in this study. Additionally, only credits given to USAS pilots while serving with USAS units are shown in Study 133, and not credits received in other air forces prior to a pilot's USAS service.

We acknowledge that there will be some who disagree with one or two of the scores in this book, while others will insist that while a final score is correct, the make-up is wrong. This is, in many cases, due to the passage of time, possibly incorrect data being acknowledged many years ago and perpetuated, or simple misinterpretations of earlier information. What the reader and researcher will find here, is our best evidence although almost every claim has had some confirmation from a number of sources, so we think we can reckon on a very high percentage of accuracy. Scores for some pilots, such as Raoul Lufbery or David Putnam, have had various differing dates shown over the years for their scores. In the case of Putnam, this probably explains why his score is sometimes thought to be over 30, which obviously includes probables, duplications, etc, which have all been lumped together. This is another good reason to display the make-up of the scores, so that historians and researchers can have the complete picture.

Each pilot has this make-up shown with the various headings of date, hostile aircraft type, the allied unit the pilot was serving in when making the claim, the location of the air action or where the hostile aircraft came down, the time of the action where known, and the confirmation details.

---

Ranks in the USAS and French Air Service may need some clarification and comparison with other Allied ranks. In the British forces, a man taking command of a Flight within a Squadron generally had the appropriate rank to go with it, such as Captain in the RFC/RAF or Flight Commander in the RNAS. In the USAS, a flight commander was generally a First Lieutenant, occasionally a Captain, while a squadron commander could still hold the rank of First Lieutenant, Captain or Major.

In the USAS all pilots were commissioned, whereas American pilots in the French Air Service could remain NCOs until either commissioned by the French, or commissioned upon transfer to the USAS.

The French Air Service ranks are generally unfamiliar to British or American readers, so are listed below for clarification.

| French rank | British rank | Remarks |
|---|---|---|
| Chef de Battalion | Major | of army/infantry |
| Chef de Escadron | Major | of cavalry |
| Commandant | Major | |
| Lieutenant | Lieutenant | ie: 1st Lt USAS |
| Sous Lieutenant | 2nd Lieutenant | ie: 2nd Lt USAS |
| Adjutant Chef | Warrant Officer | |
| Adjutant | W/Officer II | |
| Marechal-des-Logis | Sergeant | of cavalry/artillery |
| Sergent | Sergeant | of army |
| Brigadier | Corporal | of cavalry/artillery |
| Caporal | Corporal | of army |

# CHAPTER ONE

## The American's Air War Over France
## 1914-1918

The first Americans to see action in the Great War were that handful of men who joined the French in the early months of the war. Because of their nationality, they had first to join the ranks of the famous French Foreign Legion, and many of those who did, saw action in the trenches with the French Army.

During the first year, there were also a number who were either keen to transfer to the French Air Service, or decided to fly rather than fight in the mud of the trenches. These were the first Americans to see any kind of air fighting once they had trained and become pilots. Some went to various French Escadrille, flying a variety of airplane types, but then in 1915 came the idea that American volunteer pilots now training in a number of training units, be amalgamated into a front line scout (fighter, or pursuit) squadron. It took some while to organise and even be approved because of the problems of American neutrality, but eventually the Lafayette Escadrille was born, known more officially by the French as N124 (N denoting that the unit was equipped with Nieuport machines).

It had a French commanding officer, Captain Georges Thenault and French flight commanders, but the men were made up of American pilots who had received their French flying Brevet and were now ready for front line war operations. The unit scored its first success in combat in May 1916 and over the next eighteen months gained undying fame not only in its actual achievements in this still comparatively early stage of the air war, but also in the romance of the whole organisation, which history has been kind enough to preserve.

News of American volunteers, wearing French uniforms and flying French airplanes, soon spread and there followed a steady stream of would-be air fighters who travelled the Atlantic to try and join the gallant band. However, one squadron can only have a certain compliment of pilots, so the Lafayette Flying Corps was formed. This allowed other Americans to join the French Air Service and if N124 was up to full strength, these other trained airmen would be assigned to alternative French fighter escadrille.

Meantime, as the war progressed, other Americans decided to join the ranks of either the British Royal Flying Corps or Royal Naval Air Service. Some joined in Canada, others coming to Britain direct. These men too were eager to fight for the Allied powers before America came into the war and a number saw action in France with British squadrons.

When finally America did join the conflict, in April 1917, the United States Air Service in its native country had started to grow but was still very much in its infancy.

---

At the beginning of April 1917, the USAS was no more than the Aviation Section of the US Signal Corps, with not a single unit having trained for air warfare. The whole Section had just 131 officers, most of whom were pilots, or students under training, and 1087 enlisted men. Of the pilots, there were just 26 who could be said to be fully trained aviators.

Airplanes were equally few in number and certainly none could be considered warplanes in the true sense of the word. However, with the American Army on the march, the Air Service prepared for war, sending advanced men to France to begin to set up the organisation. Partly trained pilots were sent to both Canada and England to further or to complete their training under the experienced eye of the Royal Flying Corps, and some were assigned to front line squadrons in order to gain front line battle experience which they could then take to new American Squadrons as they were formed and were shipped overseas.

Meantime, the first USAS squadrons were formed, mainly in Texas, the first units sailing for France in late 1917 or early 1918. Among the first was the 95th Pursuit Squadron, whose pilots completed their training at Issoudun, a famous French training base. Issoudun became the main Aviation Instruction Centre for the Americans.

Most American military pilots who saw part or all of their training in France would see some duty at the following French bases. Avord for basic training with preliminary training at Tours. Aerobatic training was undertaken at Pau and aerial gunnery at Cazaux. As the reader will see in the pilot biographies, many pilots were assigned to at least one or more of these places as they progressed to front line aviator.

The first USAS Squadrons were equipped with Nieuport 28 single-seat fighters. They were a special breed of the famous Nieuport line and became firmly associated with the first American pursuit squadrons. Few, if any, Nieuport 28s saw action with the French, but 297 were purchased by the American Expeditionary Force and the first went to the 94th and 95th Pursuit Squadrons. The Nieuport 28 was different in many ways to its predecessors such as the famous Nieuport 17 and later Nieuport 24 and 27. The main differences were in shape, for the fuselage was very much longer (by some 2-3 feet) and in place of the more familiar small-cord lower wings (28 inches), it had a more normal looking pair of lower wings (39 inches). It also had a 160 hp Gnome-Rhone Monosoupape 9N rotary engine rather than the less powerful Le Rhone engines of the 17, 24 and 27s. Its armament was two Vickers machine guns which were placed off-set to the port side of the forward fuselage — the only WWI machine to have two guns in such a configuration.

On 14th April, 1918, Lieutenants Doug Campbell and Alan Winslow of the 94th 'Hat in Ring' Squadron, downed two German scouts, the first to fall to a USAS squadron. Despite these and other early victories, the Nieuport 28 was not popular with the American pilots, for in a steep dive they tended to shed wing fabric. Several pilots experienced this which did nothing to boost confidence in an air battle. Steps were taken by the manufacturers to overcome this problem but it came too late for the American Squadrons soon began to re-equip with the more robust French Spad S.XIII fighters.

The Spad became the standard pursuit airplane for all the American squadrons, as indeed it became for the French. With a 200 hp Hispano-Suiza engine, twin Vickers machine guns, a good speed and a better ceiling than the Nieuport (23,000 ft rather than 20,000), the pilots liked it and flew it with confidence.

The first squadrons saw action on the Toul front, with the 94th and 95th daily gaining experience, while the 103rd continued to fly and fight without interruption while still under French Army command. The 103rd Squadron, in fact, the former Lafayette Escadrille, had continued at the front. It became part of the AEF in February 1918, its French trained Americans being commisioned into the USAS.

The 103rd saw action over the Champagne sector from La Noblette, then over the Aisne Sector, from Bonne Maison and finally on the Ypres/Lys front, from Dunkirk on the British part of the front. The 103rd did not, in fact, come under American control until the summer of 1918 when the 3rd Pursuit Group was formed.

The Toul Sector of Lorraine was selected for the Americans in order to give them time to gain experience, over a part of the front whch was quieter than others. It was bounded in the west by the River Meuse and to the east by the Metz-Nancy road. The front line had changed very little in three and a half years of fighting, and both the French and the Germans tended to use the sector as a rest zone. The German fighters encountered by the first USAS pilots in the Toul Sector were of the two main types for early 1918, the Albatros Scout (both the DIII and DV[a]) and Pfalz DIII, but rarely the Fokker DrI Triplane, which in any event was on the decline at this time.

Two-seat observation airplanes used by the German Air Service in early 1918 were the Albatros CIII, Halberstadt CV, Rumpler CVII and LVG CV. Front line Schutzstaffeln, later redesignated Schlachtstaffeln (battle flights) operated with the Hannover CLIIIa and Halberstadt CLIV. It is not always certain if combats with an aircraft stated to be a Halberstadt was from an observation unit or a battle flight, the latter used for escort work and army support at low level. Generally, however, Albatros, Rumpler and LVG two-seaters were all assumed to be observation or photo-reconnaissance machines.

Very gradually further American Pursuit Squadrons arrived at the front, following the usual route of the French training bases, and later units were all equipped with Spads prior to reaching the battle front. There arrived too the first USAS bombing and observations squadrons, which gave the pursuit pilots additional work in protection and escort flights as well as offensive patrols to seek out enemy patrols or observation planes working over or behind the French and American front line trenches. Again these observation and bombing squadrons used French aircraft — Breguet XIVs, Salmson 2A2s, or British DH4s, built under licence in the US and powered by the American Liberty engine.

Kite balloons, used by both sides throughout the war, were also fair game for the pursuit pilot to attack. Just as a hostile two-seat observation crew would gain information to take back to their field commanders, so too could the balloon observer spy out movements behind the Allied lines or range guns on enemy positions. To attack balloons was a highly dangerous business, for both sides tried to protect the otherwise vulnerable gas-bags. They were generally surrounded by many light anti-aircraft guns as well as machine-gun posts, and more often than not, would have a fighting air patrol nearby, ready to intercept any would-be balloon strafer. If an attack started, the balloon's ground crew would start to haul the gas-bag down rapidly, not only to try to save it but it would also lure the attacker to a lower altitude and therefore, nearer the ground defensive fire. If he felt in imminent danger, the balloon observer would jump out of his dangling basket and descend to the ground by a rudimentary parachute device.

The pursuit pilot might also, especially during a large ground offensive, be assigned to ground attack duties, usually flying in at low level to machine-gun enemy troops or positions. This could have devastating effects on the opposing soldiers but it also brought the pursuit machines dangerously low and again vulnerable to ground fire from not just AA fire but rifle fire from any soldier with a gun.

---

In March 1918 the Germans began their mighty offensive against the British front, to the north, which drove a deep salient into the British positions. This was on the Somme Sector and another thrust just a bit further north on the River Lys, south of Ypres, also pushed back the British. Although this offensive — Germany's last major effort in Flanders — petered out within a few weeks, the initial success needed to be supported.

In order to pin-down the French along their section of the front, and by so doing draw away any support the French might give to their British Allies, the Germans aimed a third strike on the Aisne Sector. Thus on 27 May 1918, 42 German divisions attacked the French along a 25-mile stretch of the front. They took Chemin-des-Dames, crossed the Aisne River and by 3rd June had reached the Marne River at Chateau Thierry — which was just 56 miles from Paris.

Here the French, supported by the 2nd and 3rd US Divisions, halted the enemy push. Although only meant as a diversion to the main battle further north, the German success on the Aisne turned it into a major offensive. Thus the Chateau Thierry battles, over which the American air squadrons fought ferociously, turned into a critical phase of the fighting on this part of the Western Front.

Along the Marne River and around Chateau Thierry, the Americans had their first real test. Units of ground and air forces moved from the Toul Sector to the Aisne-Marne Sector in June. Four squadrons of the newly formed 1st Pursuit Group, 27th, 94th, 95th and 147th Squadrons, under Major Bert M Atkinson, with three squadrons of the I Corps Observation Group, came under the command of Colonel Billy Mitchell's 1st Brigade. On the other side of the lines, were more experienced and battle hardened German fighter units, supporting the offensive. So the American pursuit pilots began to engage better German pilots in air combat.

While the American troops on the ground fought at places which gained prominence in American folk lore — Belleau Wood and Chateau Thierry itself — the airmen fought equally bitter battles with their German counterparts in the sky above.

The heavy fighting continued through July until, in early August the Germans were finally forced back, squeezed between Reims and Soissons, until they fell back to high ground north of the Vesle River, which brought the offensive to an end. The 1st Pursuit Group had fought well and hard, claiming 38 enemy planes downed but losing 36 of their own pilots. The nucleus of the group went on to help expand the growing USAS strength for the final battles of the war.

For five weeks following the Aisne-Marne battles, there was a lull, during which time there had been a drastic reorganisation of both American land and air forces, as a prelude to the first major American offensive. Having proved themselves in the field, the promised plan for an independent American Army in France under General Pershing, now came to fruition. The Americans were now assigned to make a huge offensive in the St Mihiel Sector, just to the south of Verdun.

During the period of the build-up, the 2nd Pursuit Group was formed, on 29 July, at Toul. It was commanded by Major Davenport Johnson, a former commanding officer of the 95th Aero, consisting of two new units, the 13th and 139th Squadrons, plus the experienced 103rd — better known as the old Lafayette Escadrille (N124). Meantime, a short distance away, at Vaucouleurs, the 3rd Pursuit Group was being formed under the leadership of the former CO of the Lafayette Squadron, Major Bill Thaw.

By the middle of August, the two Groups were set. The 2nd Group now consisted of the 13th, 22nd, 49th and 139th Squadrons, while the 3rd Group had the 28th, 93rd, 103rd and 213rd Aeros. Also in this month, the 1st Group had a change of leadership, Atkinson making way for Major H E Hartney, former CO of the 27th Pursuit Squadron.

The 1st Pursuit Group continued operations on the Chateau Thierry front in August, while the other two Groups, virtually all inexperienced except for the veteran 103rd, hurriedly trained for the battle which was due to begin in September. The 2nd Group began operations in the Toul area at the end of June, its pilots too hoping to gain all the knowledge and experience they could.

The St Mihiel Offensive began on 12 September 1918, the air service airplanes supporting the American 42nd 'Rainbow' Division who were to spearhead the assault. American reconnaissance pilots supported the attack and in turn were supported and protected by US pursuit squadrons. Billy Mitchell had under his command some 1,500 French and American aircraft, Mitchell having persuaded the French to commit most of the units in this Sector to his plan.

For this assault on the enemy lines, Davenport Johnson's 2nd Pursuit Group was at Toul on the eastern flank, Thaw's 3rd Group was at Vaucouleurs, to the south west of Toul, while Hartney's 1st Group operated from Rembercourt on the Western part of the St Mihiel line.

Opposing the Americans were experienced Jasta pilots flying Fokker DVII fighters, and indeed, from now till the war's end, these deadly Fokker biplanes would be the main adversary of the US squadrons. The air battles raged above St Mihiel, Thiaucourt, Chambley, Pont-a-Mousson, Mars-la-Tour and the heights of the Moselle River.

Within a week, the Americans were facing crack German squadrons, such as the old Richthofen Circus — Jagdgeschwader No.1 with Jastas 4, 6, 10, 11 then JG2's Jastas 12, 13, 15 and 19.

By 26th September the St Mihiel fighting had been won and the final Meuse-Argonne offensive was launched. This was to the north of St Mihiel, a few miles further north than Verdun. Now the Americans were fighting over Bayonville, Damvillers, Montfaucon, St Juvin and Stenay.

Along a 20-mile front, dominated still by the north to south ridge of the valley of the Meuse, while further west was the valley of the River Aire, the attack began. It was rugged country, dominated by the ridges and the heavily wooded Argonne Forest. It was these natural defence positions that General Pershing's three army corps would have to attack and capture. Progress was slow and the fighting intense. Billy Mitchell, now a brigadier general, had 800 aircraft at his disposal, three-quarters of them American. The pilots, who had now mostly seen action at Chateau Thierry and certainly at St Mihiel, had gained in the vital experience needed to stay alive in combat. But the opposition in the air was just as experienced and the air fighting was bitter, with heavy casualties on both sides.

Hartney's 1st Group was handed the job of clearing the enemy balloon lines and low-level attack aircraft, while the other two Groups kept the upper air free from enemy airplanes and flew escort missions to bombers. This offensive lasted through three main phases, into October and then November. In late October the 4th Pursuit Group was formed, comprising the 141st, 25th, 17th and 148th Squadrons, commanded by Major Charles J Biddle. The latter two units had been under British control (65th Wing RAF) for much of the summer and now transferred to American command. Only the 141st managed to see some action before the war ended on 11th November.

When the war did end, most of the enemy positions assigned to the American ground troops had been taken on the front, as a million GI's inched their way forward against a determined German army. The Argonne Forest was cleared and the battle went forward to the east of the Meuse. To the right of the line, between Verdun and Pont-a-Mousson, the fight also continued till the end. Then came the morning of 11th November 1918, and the guns finally fell silent after four years three months, with victory to the Allied side.

The first victory scored by a USAS airman in the Great War had fallen to Lieutenant Stephen W Thompson, an observer with the 1st Observation Squadron. On 5th February 1918, he volunteered to fly with a French unit on a raid to Saarbrucken, flying in a Breguet. Attacked by German Albatros Scouts, Thompson had shot one down from his rear cockpit, although it took nearly 50 years to have the victory confirmed. The first victory by a USAS 'pilot' was, of course, scored by Douglas Campbell of the 94th Aero, on 14th April, 1918. The last victory was claimed by Major Maxwell Kirby, flying with the same 94th Aero Squadron. He shot down a Fokker DVII at 10.50 am on the morning of 10th November, just 24 hours short of the cease fire.

# CHAPTER TWO

## The American Squadrons

At the end of each brief unit history a list is given of the pilots who gained five or more victories, or became an ace flying with that unit or scored initial victories with it. Where a higher figure is given in brackets after the number of victories quoted, this relates to that individual's total claims for the war.

### 13th Pursuit Squadron

Arrived in France in June 1918. Became part of the US 2nd Pursuit Group when this was formed at Toul on 29 July 1918 (with 139th, 22nd and 49th Squadrons). The CO was Captain Charles J Biddle, who helped to score the unit's first victory on 1st August. Flew Spad aircraft, whose insignia was that of a running skeleton brandishing a bloody scythe — 'The Grim Reaper'. It was officially credited with 29 victories but no balloons.

| | | | | | |
|---|---|---|---|---|---|
| Lt M.K. Guthrie | 6 | Lt W.H. Stovall | 6 | Lt J.J. Seerley | 5 |
| Lt F.K. Hays | 6 | Maj C.J. Biddle | 5(7) | | |

### 17th Pursuit Squadron

Formed in the USA in 1917, this unit was sent to France where it entered action in July 1918, flying British Sopwith Camels, as part of the British 65th Wing. Later, under III Brigade, the squadron took part in the August offensive, while in September many low flying ground attack sorties were flown. In October, the 17th Aero was posted to the American front to join the 4th Pursuit Group but the war ended before it got into action. 53 aircraft were claimed shot down with 11 more 'out of control', but losses included 13 pilots killed and six more taken prisoner. Six Camels were lost in a single action with JG III on 26 August. Carried the RAF markings — a white dumbell.

| | | | | | |
|---|---|---|---|---|---|
| Lt H. Burdick | 8 | Lt G.A. Vaughn | 6(13) | Lt R.M. Todd | 5 |
| Lt H.C. Knotts | 6 | Lt L.A. Hamilton | 5(10) | Lt W.D. Tipton | 3(5) |

### 22nd Pursuit Squadron

Had originally been scheduled as a De Havilland 4 bombing squadron, several of its pilots having been trained with RAF De Havilland units. This was changed in July 1918 and by mid-August it had been equipped with Spad XIIIs. Commanded by Captain Raymond C. Bridgeman (who scored 4 victories) who had been with the 139th Squadron, the 22nd made its first war patrols on 16 August. Lt Arthur Brooks scored its first victory on 2 September and in all it was given credit for 44 airplane victories plus 2 balloons. Its insignia was a firey comet in a circle of stars and in September, it became part of the 2nd Pursuit Group.

| | | | | | |
|---|---|---|---|---|---|
| Capt J.M. Swaab | 10 | Capt A.R. Brooks | 6 | Lt R. DeB Vernam | 5(6) |
| Lt J.D. Beane | 8 | | | | |

### 27th Pursuit Squadron

Formed at Kelly Field as Company 'K' on 8 May 1917. Redesignated the 21st Provisional Aero Squadron on 15 June, it then became the 27th Aero on 23 July. Overseas early 1918, England, then France and finally, at Epiez. It then became part of the 1st Pursuit Group at Toul on 1 June 1918. Commanded by Major Harold E. Hartney, a veteran of the British RFC, and later by Captain Alfred S. Grant (who scored two official victories). Began operations on 2 June and on the 13th, scored its first success and sustained its first loss. Credited with 34 victories, plus 22 balloons. Its insignia was that of an American Eagle.

| | | | | | |
|---|---|---|---|---|---|
| Lt F. Luke Jr | 18 | Lt D. Hudson | 6 | Capt J.C. Vasconcells | 6 |
| Lt J.F. Wehner | 6 | Lt J.D. MacArthur | 6 | Maj H.E. Hartney | 1(7) |

### 28th Pursuit Squadron

First activated at Kelly Field, San Antonio, Texas on 10 May 1917 and designated the 28th Aero on 22 June. CO was Captain J.R. Alfonte and on 14 July, Major P. Frissell. To Canada in August, later returned to Fort Worth, Texas, under Major C.A. Browne. Squadron sailed for England in February, 1918 and went to France in March, becoming part of Bill Thaw's 3rd Pursuit Group. Commanded now by Captain C. Maury Jones, who had been a flight commander with the 13th Aero, it began operations on 2 September, flying Spad XIIIs in the St Mihiel offensive. The unit's insignia was that of a Red Indian's head bearing a single feather. First victory scored on 14 September and in all, the unit shot down 15 airplanes but no balloons.

| Lt M. Stenseth | 7 | Capt T.G. Cassady | 4(9) |
|---|---|---|---|

## 49th Pursuit Squadron

Commanded by Lt George F. Fisher, it was part of the 2nd Pursuit Group together with the 13th, 22nd and 139th Squadrons. First victory scored on 14 September 1918; total credits 24 enemy aircraft but no balloons. The squadron produced no aces, Lt David H. Backus, Lt Hugh L. Fontaine and Lt James F. Manning being top scorers with 4 victories apiece. Flew Spad XIIIs with a snarling wolf's head insignia.

## 93rd Pursuit Squadron

Part of Thaw's 3rd Pursuit Group. Commanded by Major John Huffer, who had seen service with the French, it began operations from its base at Vaucouleurs on 11 August 1918. First victory claimed on 12 September and in total, claimed 31 airplanes and one balloon. Flew Spad XIIIs and carried a Red Indian's head insignia, with two feathers in forelock. Later CO was Captain Robert Rockwell, formally CO of the 103rd Aero.

| Lt C.E. Wright | 9 | Lt L.J. Rummel | 7 | Lt C.R. D'Olive | 5 |
|---|---|---|---|---|---|

## 94th Pursuit Squadron

Formed at Kelly Field 10 August 1917, trained and reached France early in 1918. Activated at Villeneuve in March, flying French Nieuport 28s when it became operational under the command of Major Raoul Lufbery and later Major John Huffer. First two victories scored on 14 April. Later re-equipped with Spad XIIIs. Insignia was Uncle Sam's hat in a circle, denoting Uncle Sam's hat thrown in the ring. It thus became known as the 'Hat in Ring' Squadron. Was given official credit for 54 victories and 13 balloons. In July, Captain Kenneth Marr took command and in September, Captain Eddie Rickenbacker.

| Capt E.V. Rickenbacker | 26 | Lt H.W. Cook | 7 | Lt J.A. Meissner | 4(6) |
|---|---|---|---|---|---|
| Capt H. Coolidge | 8 | Lt D. Campbell | 6 | Maj G.R. Lufbery | −(16) |
| Capt R.M. Chambers | 7 | Capt D. Mc Peterson | 5(6) | | |

## 95th Pursuit Squadron

Activated at Kelly Field, Texas, 20 August 1917. Went overseas late September arriving at Issoudun on 16 November to prepare for active duty. It was commanded by Captain J.J. Miller, going to Villeneuve on 18 February. While waiting for its compliment of Nieuport 28 aircraft, Miller and two other pilots borrowed three Spads and flew a patrol but Miller was shot down by German aircraft and killed. The new CO was Major Davenport Jones and then in June, Major David Peterson took over. Re-equipped with Spad XIIIs, it was part of the 1st Pursuit Group at Rembercourt. Final victory tally of 35 airplanes plus 12 balloons. Its insignia was that of a kicking mule.

| Lt L.C. Holden | 7 | Lt E.P. Curtis | 6 | Lt J. Knowles | 5 |
|---|---|---|---|---|---|
| Lt S. Sewell | 7 | Lt H.E. Buckley | 5 | Capt D. Mc Peterson | −(6) |

## 103rd Pursuit Squadron

Formed from personnel of N124 — the Lafayette Escadrille, on February 1918 and remained with the Groupe de Chasse 21 until 10 April. First CO was Major William Thaw; unit pilots, of course, were all French trained. Later commanded by Captain Robert Rockwell. Came under US control on 1 July 1918, still flying Spads and became part of the 3rd Pursuit Group — with the 28th, 93rd and 213rd Aero Squadrons. Given credit for 47 victories plus two balloons, it carried the famous Indian Chief's head insignia that the Lafayette aircraft had on its Nieuports.

| Lt P.F. Baer | 9 | Lt G.W. Furlow | 5 | Maj W. Thaw | 3(5) |
|---|---|---|---|---|---|
| Lt F.O'D. Hunter | 8 | Lt G. deF Larner | 5(7) | Maj C. Biddle | 1(7) |
| Lt E.G. Tobin | 6 | Lt W.T. Ponder | 3(6) | | |

## 139th Pursuit Squadron

Activated at Kelly Field, Texas, 21 September 1917, training at the British Taliaferro Field, near Fort Worth. Commanded by Major Lawrence C. Angstrom, the unit went overseas, arriving in England on 5 March 1918. Completed training in England and then Tours, France, equipped with Spad XIIIs at Vaucouleurs. On 30 June it became part of the 2nd Pursuit Group. The veteran David Putnam, who had been successful with the French, claimed the unit's first victories on the same day. Putnam also took temporary command of the unit when Angstrom was ill. Credited with 34 victories but no balloons. A flying Mercury figure was the Squadron's insignia.

| Lt W.A. Robertson | 7 | Lt H.H. George | 5 | Capt D.E. Putnam | 4(13) |
| Lt K.J. Schoen | 7 | Lt E.M. Haight | 5 | | |
| Lt R.O. Lindsay | 6 | Lt J.S. Owens | 5 | | |

## 141st Pursuit Squadron

Began operations from Toul Airdrome on 23 October 1918, flying Spad XIIIs, in support of the US Second Army. It was commanded by Captain Hobart A.H. Baker, the famous Princeton athlete, who had been a flight commander with the 103rd. He claimed the unit's first victory on the 28th but it only accounted for two airplanes before hostilities ceased on 11 November. The Squadron's insignia was a tiger playing with a spiked German helmet. 'Hobe' Baker was killed in a flying accident in December 1918.

## 147th Pursuit Squadron

Activated in the US in November 1917, it trained and went to England, then over to France. At Epiez it became part of the 1st Pursuit Group, along with the 27th, 94th and 95th Squadrons. Flying Spad XIIIs, its insignia was a ratting terrier. Its official victory score was 28 airplanes, plus three balloons. Commanded by Major Geoffrey H. Bonnell, who had seen service with the British RFC gaining at least one victory with 32 Squadron, and later Captain James A. Meissner, late of the 94th Aero, the unit first scored on 2 July.

| Lt W.W. White | 8 | Lt K.L. Porter | 6 | Lt F.M. Simonds | 5 |
| Lt R. O'Neill | 6 | Lt J.A. Healy | 5 | Capt J.A. Meissner | 4(8) |

## 148th Pursuit Squadron

Formed at Kelly Field, Texas, late 1917, the unit was posted to France where it began operations under British control on 20 July 1918. However, some patrols had been flown earlier and the Squadron gained its first success on 13 July. The unit moved to the American front on 29 October but was too late to see further action before the war ended. It was credited with 47 airplanes destroyed with another 19 driven down out of control. Carried RAF identification insignia — a white triangle.

| Capt E.W. Springs | 12(16) | Lt J.O. Creech | 8 | Lt L.K. Callahan | 2(5) |
| Capt F.E. Kindley | 11(12) | Capt C.L. Bissell | 5 | | |
| Lt H.R. Clay Jr | 8 | Lt A.O. Ralston | 3(5) | | |

## 213rd Pursuit Squadron

Commanded by Lieutenant John Hamilton, who had earlier been wounded with the 95th Aero, it was equipped with Spad XIIIs. Began operations on 14 August 1918, as part of the 3rd Pursuit Group, with the 93rd, 29th and 103rd Squadrons. Officially credited with 15 victories and one balloon, it produced just one ace. Its first victory was scored on 21 August and its planes carried yet another variation of a Red Indian's head insignia, in full warpaint and a single feather.

| Capt C.G. Gray | 5 |

## 185th Pursuit Squadron

Commanded by Lieutenant Seth Low and in the final days of the war by Captain Jerry Vasconcells, this was the only night fighter unit the USAS had in France. Equipped with British Sopwith Camels, it was based on the St Mihiel front, attached to the 1st Pursuit Group. Its pilots flew several night patrols but scored no official victories. However, the Group Commander, Colonel H.E. Hartney, flew a night sortie on 22 October, engaging a Gotha bomber. Although he attacked several times he made no claim but after the war the bullet-ridden remains of a Gotha was found in the area of the combat and may well have been Hartney's 7th victory and the 185th's first and only, had he made a claim! The airplanes carried a bat emblem in a circle.

| Capt J. Vasconcells | –(6) | Maj H.E. Hartney | –(6) |

The Following American Pilots Flew Solely With Either British Or French Squadrons To Achieve Acedom

| | | |
|---|---|---|
| Blair Lt H.L. | 24 Sqdn RAF | SE5A |
| Beaver Capt W. | 20 Sqdn RFC/RAF | BF2b |
| Bennett Jr Lt L. | 40 Sqdn RAF | SE5A |
| Bissonette Lt C.A. | 64 Sqdn RAF | SE5A |
| Boyson Lt H.K. | 66 Sqdn RFC/RAF | Sopwith Camel |
| Brown Lt S.M. | 29 Sqdn RAF | SE5A |
| Buchanan Lt A. | 210 Sqdn RAF | Sopwith Camel |
| Callender Capt A.A. | 32 Sqdn RAF | SE5A |
| Catto Lt C.G. | 45 Sqdn RAF | Sopwith Camel |
| Coler Lt E.S. | 11 Sqdn RAF | BF2b |
| Cooper Lt N. | 73 Sqdn RAF | Sopwith Camel |
| Donaldson Capt J.O. | 32 Sqdn RAF | SE5A |
| Gillet Capt F.W. | 79 Sqdn RAF | Sopwith Dolphin |
| Griffiths Lt J.S. | 60 Sqdn RAF | SE5A |
| Hale Capt F.L. | 32 Sqdn RAF | SE5A |
| Hilton Lt D'A.F. | 29 Sqdn RAF | SE5A |
| Howell Lt M.G. | 208 Sqdn RAF | Sopwith Camel |
| Iaccaci Lt A.T. | 20 Sqdn RAF | BF2b |
| Iaccaci Lt P.T. | 20 Sqdn RAF | BF2b |
| Ingalls Lt D.S. | 213 Sqdn RAF | Sopwith Camel |
| Knight Lt D. | 1 Sqdn RAF | SE5A |
| Kullberg Capt H.A. | 1 Sqdn RAF | SE5A |
| Lambert Capt W.C. | 24 Sqdn RAF | SE5A |
| Landis Maj R.G. | 40 Sqdn RAF | SE5A |
| Larsen Lt J.F. | 84 Sqdn RAF | SE5A |
| LeBoutillier Capt O.C. | 9/209 RNAS/RAF | Sopwith Triplane and Camel |
| Libby Capt F. | 23/11 Sqdns RFC | FE2b |
| ,, | 43 Sqdn RFC | Sopwith 1½ Strutter |
| ,, | 25 Sqdn RFC | DH4 |
| Lord Capt F.I. | 79 Sqdn RAF | Sopwith Dolphin |
| Luff Lt F.E. | 74 Sqdn RAF | SE5A |
| Lussier Capt E.J. | 73 Sqdn RAF | Sopwith Camel |
| Magoun Lt F.P. | 1 Sqdn RFC/RAF | SE5A |
| Pearson Capt J.W. | 23 Sqdn RAF | Sopwith Dolphin |
| Pineau Lt C.F. | 210 Sqdn RAF | Sopwith Camel |
| Rogers Lt B. | 32 Sqdn RAF | SE5A |
| Rose Capt O.J. | 92 Sqdn RAF | SE5A |
| Simon Lt W.K. | 139 Sqdn RAF | BF2b |
| Taylor Lt E. | 79 Sqdn RAF | Sopwith Dolphin |
| Unger Lt K.R. | 210 Sqdn RAF | Sopwith Camel |
| Warman Capt C.W. | 23 Sqdn RFC | Spad |
| White Lt H.A. | 23 Sqdn RAF | Sopwith Dolphin |
| | | |
| Baylies Lt F.L. | Spa3 | Spad |
| Connelly Jr Adj J.A. | Spa157/Spa163 | Spad |
| Lufbery Maj G.R. | N124 | Nieuport |
| Parsons Lt E.C. | N124/Spa3 | Nieuport Scout/Spad |

# Interpretation of the Claim Lists

Just a few words are necessary to explain the following claim lists appended to each pilot biography.

Reading from left to right, the first column indicates the numerical sequence of the pilot's claims/credits, running from one onwards. Where there is a remark concerning this victory, either due to it being a shared victory, or perhaps the victim has been positively identified, etc, it is followed by a bracketed letter, e.g. (a), (b), etc. For an explanation of this letter, the reader should refer to the notes at the end of each claim list.

The next column indicates the date of the victory, shown under year and then day and month. The third column shows the type of enemy aircraft the pilot or gunner claimed. As is generally known by the aviation historian or enthusiast, with an aeroplane with the classification C (e.g. LVG CV), the 'C' indicates it was a two-seater. With CL (e.g. Halberstadt CLIII) this indicates a two-seater fighter or ground attack aeroplane. A 'D' (e.g. Albatros DIII), indicates a single-seat biplane scout, or fighter, a 'Dr' (e.g. Fokker Dr1), a triplane fighter, and an 'E' (e.g. Fokker EIII), a monoplane.

The number in column four represents the squadron or squadrons in which the airman served when scoring that particular victory. Most pilots in WW1 tended to remain with a single unit, until perhaps promotion made it necessary to transfer or be posted to another unit. Or perhaps a return to the front after a period of rest; he might also be assigned to another unit. In any event, the number in the column shows the number of the unit(s). It will be noted that with French Escadrille (squadrons) a designation, e.g. N3 will change to Spa3. This is exactly the same escadrille but the letter changed when the aeroplane type changed, in this case, from Nieuport to Spad. However, the designation was not always made official with the change over of equipment, so that an escadrille flying new Spads might still be officially designated as N—, rather than Spa—, for a while. For a check on the aeroplane type used, the reader should refer to the unit histories.

The fifth column shows the location of the combat, which could be either the approximate area above which the action was fought, or the spot where the hostile aeroplane fell. The sixth column records the time (although sometimes only the approximate time) the combat took place — when known/recorded.

In cases where an American pilot flew wholly or for a time with either the Royal Flying Corps, Royal Air Force or Royal Naval Air Service, and received official credit for a 'victory' with these forces, there is a column which may show a destroyed victory (DES), an 'out of control' victory (OOC), or an aircraft brought down inside Allied lines and captured (CAPT). As already mentioned in the introduction, because these types of victories were credited with the RFC, RAF, RNAS, they are shown as such in these claim lists.

The final column records the confirmation record: the official recognition of the victory claimed. In the case of French victories, these generally would only be accepted as official if they appeared in the Communiques, on the date the victory was confirmed — which might be different from the day it was claimed. i.e. it may be several days or even weeks before a claim was made official. The Communiques were numbered, therefore, the column may, for example, be noted as in the case of the second victory of Bernard Artigau, of N15:

| 2 | 1 Nov (1917) 2-seater | Chevrigny | 1245 | 12 Nov | 12.908 |

This shows that his claim of 1st November, was not actually confirmed until 12th November as noted in Communique No. 12.908.

Or, perhaps, confirmation has been found elsewhere, as in the case of the second victory of Maurice Arnoux of Spa49:

| 2 | 8 June (1918) Balloon | Ferrette | 0946 | 9 Jun | 5.656 |

This is shown in the claim list as being the date (one day later than on which it was claimed!) recorded in the VII Armee Compte Rendu des Operations Aerienne. (Report of aerial operations by units under the command of the 8th French Army.)

Other similar alternative confirmation reports, such as those which subsequently appeared in medal citations, are also duly noted where they are shown.

With the squadrons of the United States Air Service, in the initial weeks of the American units being at the front, their victories too appeared in the French Communiques as shown in the claim lists. Once the USAS HQ had taken full responsibilites for their units, confirmations appearded in General Orders (GOs). Thus, for example, the first victory of Ray Brooks of the 139th and 22nd Pursuit Squadrons was noted in a French Communique, whereas the third is noted in (US) General Orders No.5:

| 1 | 29 Jul | Pfalz DIII | Heudicourt | 3 Aug | 5.172 |
| 3 | 4 Sep | Fokker DVII | Barnecourt | | GO 5 |

It will be noted that in the latter case, there is no differing date shown as the confirmation in whatever 'GO' always referred to the date of the claim.

Any variation in the source of the confirmation, such as a claim being mentioned in USAF 133 (a listing of American fighter credits made by the Academy at Maxwell Air Force Base, Alabama), is noted at the end of the claim list text.

Confirmation by the RFC, RAF and RNAS is very different. Although they used Communiques, these were merely for the dissemination of information to all operational units; more of a morale booster than an 'official' recognition of anything. As the British never gave official recognition to their 'aces' they, of course, did not record each and every pilot or gunner's score in any form of running total. Therefore, the confirmation is a little more ambiguous and they have merely been taken from all sorts of reports in addition to those which may have also been mentioned in the Communiques. Therefore, reference to CR/RAF, means that a Combat Report has been located which may also appear to have been noted as being confirmed as a claim, and that the victory has been shown in the RAF Communique. Other assumed confirmations may appear in a War Diary (WD), a citation, or a Wing Report.

# CHAPTER THREE

# The American Aces — Biographical and Claim Notes

## BADHAM William Terry      Lieutenant      AR214, BR40 AND 210, 91ST AERO

Born Birmingham, Alabama, 27 September 1895, this officer served as an Observer/gunner in three French Escadrille, AR214 flying Dorand AR1's during April and May 1918, then BR40 and BR210 who operated with Breguets. Finally he was reassigned to the American 91st Observation Squadron which operated with Salmson 2A2s. On 12 June he and his pilot, Lt Willis A. Diekema had a lucky escape when engaged by anti-aircraft fire over Arneville. The machine was hit some thirty times and the radiator was punctured. Diekema also had a piece of shell fragment cut a furrow through his flying helmet! Luckily they got back over the lines before the engine gave out. Badham's pilot when he scored his first victory was Lieutenant George C. Kenny who in WWII would command the US 5th Air Force in the Far East for part of the war. The pilot for his next four victories was the units' CO, Captain Everett R. Cook. In air combat, Badham was credited with shooting down five German fighters and he received the DSC. After WWI worked in his father's coal mining business; later formed the Naphthalene Products Co. Died Mentone, Alabama, 6 June 1991.

### DSC CITATION

For extraordinary heroism in action near Buzancy, France, 25 October 1918. This officer gave proof of exceptional bravery while on a photographic mission 25 kilometers within the enemy lines. His plane was attacked by a formation of 30 aircraft; by skilful work with his machine-gun, Lt Badham successfully repelled the attack and destroyed two German planes. At the same time he manoeuvred his camera and obtained photographs of great military value.

|       | 1918   |             |    |             |      |       |
|-------|--------|-------------|----|-------------|------|-------|
| 1(a)  | 15 Sep | Pfalz DIII  | 91 | NW Gorze    | 1140 | GO 13 |
| 2(b)  | 23 Oct | Fokker DVII | 91 | Andevanne   | 1120 | GO 21 |
| 3(b)  | 23 Oct | Pfalz DIII  | 91 | Andevanne   | 1120 | GO 21 |
| 4(b)  | 28 Oct | Fokker DVII | 91 | Malancourt  | 1620 | GO 22 |
| 5(b)  | 29 Oct | Fokker DVII | 91 | Grand Pre   | 1305 | GO 22 |

(a) Pilot, Lt G.E. Kenny; (b) Pilot, Capt E.R. Cook.

## BAER Paul Frank      1st Lieutenant      SPA80, 103RD AERO

From Fort Wayne, Indiana, born 29 January 1895. Joined the Lafayette Flying Corps in 1917 and after training was sent to the French Escadrille Spa80 on 14 August where he stayed until 10 January 1918 when he went to N124. On 18 February 1918, this unit became the American 103rd Pursuit Squadron. Baer scored the first victory for the 103rd Aero on 11 March, which was also the first victory for the USAS. He continued to fly with the Squadron until 22 May when he was shot down near Armentieres, moments after gaining his 9th victory, to become a prisoner. It is believed he was brought down, seriously wounded, by either Ltn Hans Muller (who gained his 5th of 12 victories this day) or Vzfw Debenitz both of Jasta 18. Baer received the DSC with Oak Leaf Cluster, and the French Croix de Guerre. On 9 April 1919 he became a Chevalier de la Legion d'Honneur. He was killed in an airplane crash in Hong Kong Harbour on 9 December 1930. In addition to his official 9 kills, he was credited with at least seven probable victories, four in March, three in April.

### DSC CITATION

On 11 March 1918, alone attacked a group of seven enemy pursuit machines, destroying one which crashed to the ground near the French lines northeast of Reims. On 16 March, he attacked two enemy two-seaters, one of which fell in flames, striking the ground in approximately the same region.

### BRONZE OAK LEAF CITATION

For the following repeated acts of extraordinary heroism in action 5, 12 and 23 April, 8 and 21 May 1918, Lt Baer is awarded a Bronze Oak Leaf to be worn on the Distinguished Service Cross awarded him 12 April 1918. Lt Baer brought down enemy planes on 6 April, 12 April and 23 April 1918. On 8 May 1918 he destroyed two German machines and on 21 May he destroyed his eighth enemy plane.

|      | 1918   |             |     |                    |      |        |      |
|------|--------|-------------|-----|--------------------|------|--------|------|
| 1    | 11 Mar | Albatros D  | 103 | Cerney-les-Reims   |      | 12.474 | 11/3 |
| 2    | 16 Mar | Albatros C  | 103 | Nogent l'Abbesse   |      | 23.474 | 21/3 |
| 3    | 6 Apr  | Scout       | 103 | Somme-Py           | 1855 | 6.546  | 6/4  |
| 4    | 12 Apr | Albatros D  | 103 | Proyart            | 1217 | 13.111 | 12/4 |
| 5(a) | 23 Apr | Albatros C  | 103 | St Gobain          | 0955 | 25.915 | 23/4 |
| 6    | 8 May  | Two-seater  | 103 | Mont Kemmel        | 1028 | 10.679 | 8/5  |

| 7 | 8 May | Scout | 103 | Mont Kemmel | 1738 | 10.679 | 8/5 |
| 8(b) | 21 May | Albatros | 103 | W of Ypres | 1850 | 30* | 23/5 |
| 9 | 22 May | Albatros | 103 | Laventie | 0945 | GO 5 | 1/28/1 |

(a) Shared with Lt C.H. Wilcox; (b) Shared with Lts H.A.H. Baker, C.H. Wilcox and C.W. Ford. (*) Confirmed in DAN Bulletin.

## BAIR Hilbert Leigh     Lieutenant     24RAF, 25TH AERO

From New York City, New York, born 15 November 1894. Graduated from Cornell University School of Military Aeronautics 20 October 1917. He joined the USAS 18 July 1917, trained in Canada and Texas and was attached to the RAF for operational experience. Posted to 24 Squadron in France on 5 July 1918 he gained six victories while flying SE5As and received the British DFC on 19 September. In October he was assigned to the US 25th Aero Squadron and later received the DSC. In WWII he served as a Lieutenant Colonel in the USAAC. He died on 24 November 1985 in White Springs, New York, aged 91.

### DFC CITATION

For conspicuous bravery and skill in attacking enemy aircraft and troops on the ground. On 15 September 1918, he and another pilot attacked an enemy two-seater, which after considerable fighting they drove down and crashed near Honnecourt Wood. On 16 September, he engaged and drove down completely out of control an enemy two-seater south-east of Cambrai. On 30 August 1918, he performed brilliant and valuable work attacking and silencing an enemy battery west of Bouvincourt. When this battery re-opened fire, he again attacked it and after silencing it stampeded the battery transport. In all he has destroyed or taken part in the destruction of three enemy aircraft, besides driving down two others completely out of control. His work in attacking ground targets has been of the greatest value.

| | 1918 | | | | | | |
| --- | --- | --- | --- | --- | --- | --- | --- |
| 1(a) | 10 Aug | Fokker DVII | 24 | NE Rosieres | 0750 | OOC | CR/SR |
| 2 | 19 Aug | Fokker DVII | 24 | Fresnoy | 1130 | DES | CR/SR |
| 3(b) | 19 Aug | Fokker DVII | 24 | Fresnoy | 1130 | OOC | CR/SR |
| 4(c) | 30 Aug | Albatros C | 24 | Bus | 0630 | DES | CR/RAF |
| 5 | 8 Sep | Fokker DVII | 24 | N St Quentin | 0820 | DES | CR/RAF |
| 6(d) | 15 Sep | Hannover CL | 24 | Honnecourt Wood | 1855 | DES | CR/RAF |
| –(e) | 16 Sep | Two-seater | 24 | SE Cambrai | | citation | dd |

(a) Shared with Capt W. Selwyn, Lt T.M. Harris and Lt W.C. Lambert; (b) Shared with Capt W. Selwyn; (c) Shared with Lt H.D. Barton, Lt T.M. Harris; (d) Shared with Capt H.D. Barton; (e) Although mentioned in the citation, the two-seater was only acknowledged as driven down damaged, shared with Capt H.D. Barton, Lts W.C. Sterling and R.K. Rose.

## BAYLIES Frank Leamon     Lieutenant     SPA73, SPA3

Born New Bedford, Massachusetts, 23 September 1895 and educated at Jerih Swift High School and then the Moses Brown Preparatory School in Providence, Rhode Island. From his father's merchant business he volunteered for the US Ambulance Service, sailed for France in the SS *Lafayette* in February 1916, arriving at Bordeaux 6 March. Saw active service on the Somme, at Verdun and Argonne, then went to Serbia. Here he won the Croix de Guerre in March 1917 for evacuating wounded under fire at Monastir. Early that year a French pilot took him for a flight and in May he enlisted into the French Aviation Corps, training at Avord, Pau and Lake Cazaux, receiving his Brevet on Caudrons (No 8718) on 20 September 1917. He was assigned to Spa73 at Dunkirk on 17 November and a month (18 December) later went to the famous Spa3 Escadrille of the Storks Group. He refused a captaincy in the USAS, preferring to remain with the French, with the rank of sergeant. He finally transferred in May and became a second lieutenant. He continued to fly with the Storks until his death in action on 17 June 1918. He was shot down in combat with Triplanes of Jasta 19, by either Ltns Wilhelm Leusch or Rudolf Rienau. In both cases it was their second victories and each would gain five by the war's end. Baylies' Spad fell in flames between Rollet and Orvillers and his death was confirmed when a German airman dropped a message over the lines on 6 July. He was buried at Rollet but reinterred at the Memorial de L'Escadrille Lafayette, Parc Rue, Villeneuve L'Etang, Paris, in 1927. From the French he had received the Medaille Militaire and from the US, the Medal of the Aero Club of America.

| | 1918 | | | | | | |
| --- | --- | --- | --- | --- | --- | --- | --- |
| 1 | 19 Feb | Two-seater | Spa3 | N of Forges | 1315 | 23.401 | 20/2 |
| 2 | 7 Mar | Scout | Spa3 | NE Courtecon | | 21.578 | 19/3 |
| 3 | 16 Mar | EA | Spa3 | Chevrigny | 1735 | 6.208 | 6/4 |
| 4 | 11 Apr | Two-seater | Spa3 | Mesnil-St George | 1330 | 14.388 | 13/4 |
| 5 | 12 Apr | Scout | Spa3 | S of Moreuil | 0650 | 17.922 | 16/4 |

| 6 | 2 May | Rumpler C | Spa3 | Assinvillers | 1320 | 2.734 | 2/5 |
| 7(a) | 3 May | Two-seater* | Spa3 | Montdidier | 1725 | 4.062 | 5/5 |
| 8 | 9 May | Halberstadt C | Spa3 | Braches-Gratibus | 1930 | 12.142 | 9/5 |
| 9(b) | 10 May | Two-seater | Spa3 | Montdidier | 1725 | 14.412 | 11/5 |
| 10 | 28 May | Scout | Spa3 | Courtemarches | 0815 | 36.535 | 28/5 |
| 11 | 29 May | EA | Spa3 | Etelfay | 1815 | 38.882 | 30/5 |
| 12(c) | 31 May | EA | Spa3 | Montdidier | 1045 | 3 | 31/5 |

(a) Shared with MdL A. Dubonnet; (b) Shared with MdL Clement; (c) Shared with MdL A. Dubonnet; (*) F/Abt 245, Lts Karbe and Meuche.

---

## BEANE James Dudley      Lieutenant      SPA69, 22ND AERO

Born New York City, 20 January 1896, he lived in Concord, Massachusetts in 1909, where he attended Concord High School. Leaving school he was employed in the Department of Education at the State House, Boston, before volunteering for active duty with the US Ambulance Service. Sailed for France in June 1916 and from July 1916 through July 1917, saw duty on the Verdun front. He joined the French army in August and assigned to the Lafayette Escadrille for training. He then went to Spa69 till February 1918 when he transferred to the USAS, commissioned Second Lieutenant. On 30 June he was wounded in the left hand during an air battle, losing two fingers. He received the Croix de Guerre but returned to the front six weeks later, joining the 22nd Aero Squadron. With this unit he gained six victories before he lost his life in aerial combat near Bantheville on 30 October, shot down flying Spad No 7812 '14'. He was buried 2 km east of Brieulles-sur-Bar, and was awarded a posthumous DSC.

### CROIX DE GUERRE CITATION

He instantly made his mark in the Squadron by his courage and spirit in fighting. On 30 June 1918, while on patrol, was attacked by several enemy aircraft, and although seriously wounded (two fingers of the left hand cut off) succeeded in escaping and bringing back his disabled machine. In this instance he displayed much ability and great coolness.

### DSC CITATION

For extraordinary heroism in action near Bantheville, France, 29 October 1918. When Lt Beane's patrol was attacked by eight enemy planes (Fokker type) he dived into their midst in order to divert their attention from the other machines of his group and shot down one of the Fokkers in flames. Four other Fokkers then joined the battle, one of which was also destroyed by this officer.

---

|  | 1918 | | | | | |
| 1 | 26 Sep | Fokker DVII | 22 | Charpenty | 0730 | GO 20 |
| 2(a) | 28 Sep | Fokker DVII | 22 | Ivoiry | 0840 | GO 20 |
| 3(b) | 9 Oct | DFW C | 22 | Aincreville | 1435 | GO 23 |
| 4(c) | 10 Oct | Fokker DVII | 22 | Bayonville | 1402 | GO 23 |
| 5 | 29 Oct | Fokker DVII | 22 | Ramonville | 1610 | GO 27 |
| 6(d) | 29 Oct | Fokker DVII | 22 | Aincreville | 1620 | GO 27 |

(a) Shared with Capt R.C. Bridgeman; (b) Shared with Lts A.R. Brooks and C. Jones; (c) Shared with Lt J.C. Crissey; (d) Shared with Lt R. deB Vernam.

---

## BEAVER Wilfred      Captain      20 RAF

An American citizen living in Montreal, Canada, he joined the RFC and went to 20 Squadron in late 1917, flying Bristol F2b two-seater fighters. He was awarded the MC, Gazetted 22 June 1918, became a flight commander and claimed 19 victories in company with his rear-seat gunner/observers. His main back-seaters were Lt H.E. Easton, Sgt E.A. Deighton and Cpl Mather.

### MC CITATION

For conspicuous gallantry and devotion to duty. During the last five months he has destroyed five hostile machines and has brought down completely out of control, six others. During the recent operations he has performed exceptionally good work in bombing and firing upon hostile troops from very low altitudes. He has displayed marked gallantry and resource and has proved himself a patrol leader of great dash and ability.

---

|  | 1917 | | | | | | |
| 1(a) | 13 Nov | Albatros DV | 20 | SE Houthoulst | 1500 | DES | CR/RFC |
| 2(b) | 2 Dec | Albatros DIII | 20 | SE Passchendaele | 1030 | DES | CR/RFC |
| 3(b) | 5 Dec | Albatros C | 20 | Dadizeele | 0925 | OOC | CR/RFC |

| | 1918 | | | | | | |
|---|---|---|---|---|---|---|---|
| 4(c) | 3 Jan | Albatros C | 20 | NE Moorslede | 1545 | DES | CR/RFC |
| 5(c) | 6 Jan | Albatros C | 20 | Houthoulst Forest | 1210 | OOC | CR/RFC |
| 6(c) | 3 Feb | Albatros DV | 20 | Roulers-Menin Rd | 1245 | DES | CR/RFC |
| 7(c) | 4 Feb | Albatros DV | 20 | Roulers | 1415 | OOC | Summary |
| 8(c) | 5 Feb | Albatros DV | 20 | Roulers | 1120 | OOC | CR/RFC |
| 9(c) | 5 Feb | Albatros DV | 20 | Roulers | 1122 | OOC | CR/RFC |
| 10(c) | 16 Feb | Two-seater | 20 | Menin | 1140 | OOC | CR/RFC |
| 11(c) | 23 Mar | Albatros DV | 20 | Menin-S Roncq | 1220 | DES | CR/RFC |
| 12(b) | 25 Apr | Albatros DV | 20 | N Ploegsteert Wood | 1935 | DES | CR/RAF |
| 13(d) | 3 May | Albatros DV | 20 | Gheluvelt | 1330 | DES | CR/RAF |
| 14(d) | 9 May | Albatros DV | 20 | E Warneton | 1125 | DES | CR/RAF |
| 15(d) | 27 May | Albatros DV | 20 | NE Armentieres | 1125 | OOC | CR/RAF |
| 16(d) | 27 May | Fokker DrI | 20 | NE Armentieres | 1127 | DES | CR/RAF |
| 17(d) | 27 May | Fokker DrI | 20 | NE Armentieres | 1128 | DES | CR/RAF |
| 18(d) | 29 May | Fokker DrI | 20 | Bac St Maur | 1825 | DES | CR/RAF |
| 19(d) | 13 Jun | Albatros DV | 20 | NW Armentieres | 0800 | OOC | CR/RAF |

(a) Observer Lt C.J. Angelasto; (b) Observer AM/Cpl M. Mather; (c) Observer Lt H.E. Easton; (d) Observer Sgt E.A. Deighton.

## BENNETT Jr Louis     Lieutenant     40 RAF

Born 22 September 1894, in Weston, West Virginia, he was at Yale University from 1913-17. He enlisted in the RFC in Canada in October 1917, arriving in England in February 1918. After a period with No 90 Home Defence Squadron he was sent to France to join 40 Squadron, flying SE5As, going to the Flight led by one of the British top aces, George McElroy. In some ways, Bennett became the Frank Luke of the RAF, for in less than two weeks he destroyed nine balloons and shot down three aircraft. This all happened so quickly that there was no time to reward him before he was killed, on 24 August 1918. He was brought down while attacking balloons behind the German front line, by Machine Gun Detachment Nos 920 and 921, his aircraft catching fire. He jumped from his burning SE5 at about 100 feet, breaking both legs when he hit the ground. The machine gun crews took him to a dressing station but he died while his injuries were being attended to; he was buried at Wavrin. In all he had flown just 25 sorties. His father died on 16 August but news did not reach him before his own death in action.

Although no medals were awarded, there were a number of memorials to the gallant Bennett. One was a statue of George Washington, presented to Yale University by Bennett's mother in 1932, and another was an eight-foot bronze of Bennett, entitled 'The Aviator' which stands in the grounds of Linsly Military Institute, Wheeling, West Virginia, unveiled on Armistice Day 1925.

| | 1918 | | | | | | |
|---|---|---|---|---|---|---|---|
| 1 | 15 Aug | Fokker DVII | 40 | Brebieres | 1200 | OOC | CR/Air 1/1222 |
| 2(a) | 17 Aug | LVG C | 40 | E Henin-Lietard | 0740 | DES | CR/RAF |
| 3 | 17 Aug | Balloon | 40 | SE Merville | 0800 | DES | CR/Air 1/1222 |
| 4 | 19 Aug | Balloon | 40 | E Merville | 1000 | DES | CR/RAF |
| 5 | 19 Aug | Balloon | 40 | E Merville | 1010 | DES | CR/RAF |
| 6 | 19 Aug | Balloon | 40 | E Merville | 1340 | DES | CR/RAF |
| 7 | 19 Aug | Balloon | 40 | E Merville | 1341 | DES | CR/RAF |
| 8 | 22 Aug | Balloon | 40 | W Don | 0620 | DES | CR/RAF |
| 9 | 22 Aug | Balloon | 40 | E La Bassee | 0630 | DES | CR/RAF |
| 10 | 23 Aug | LVG C | 40 | Quierry la Mottee | 0715 | DES | CR/RAF |
| 11 | 24 Aug | Balloon | 40 | Provin | 1225 | DES | CR/Air 1/1222 |
| 12 | 24 Aug | Balloon | 40 | Hantay | 1230 | DES | CR/Air 1/1222 |

(a) Shared with Lt F.H. Knobel.

## BIDDLE Charles John     Major     SPA73, N124, 103RD AND 13TH AERO

From Philadelphia, PA, he was born 13 May 1890 in Andalusia, Pennsylvania. Graduated from Princeton University in 1911 and then from Harvard in 1914. He was admitted to the Pennsylvanian Bar and except for his war service, practised law all his life. He joined the French Air Service on 8 April 1917, trained at Avord, Pau and Le Plessis-Belleville, being then assigned to the French Spa73 Escadrille on 28 July, attaining the rank of sergent. Became a member of the USAS on 7 November, commissioned as captain, but remained with his French unit until 10 January 1918. Going to N124 which then became the 103rd Pursuit Squadron in February, he flew until wounded over St Jean on 15 May, when attacking a two-seater. He returned to the front as CO of the 13th Aero on 22 June, bringing his score to seven (he also had three unconfirmed victories) by 24 October, on which date he took command of the 4th Pursuit Group, comprising the 17th, 148th, 25th and 141st squadrons. However, the war ended before the 4th could get into action as a unit. For his service he received the DSC, Purple Heart, the French Legion d'Honneur (9 April 1919) and Croix de Guerre with three palmes (27 Jan, 29 Apr, 4 June 1918 and 17 May 1919); he also received the Belgian Order of Leopold.

### CROIX DE GUERRE CITATION (4 JUNE 1918)

Pilot of marvellous spirit. Attacked two enemy two-seaters successively behind their lines, probably shooting down the first. Wounded and disabled in the course of the second combat by sheer strength he succeeded in landing in 'no-man's-land' and after passing the day in a shell hole, by night he got back to the Allied trenches.

Released from service in 1919, he wrote *The Way of the Eagle*, then returned to law in 1924. He died in Andalusia, Bucks County, PA, on 22 March 1972, aged 81.

|  | 1917 |  |  |  |  |  |  |
|---|---|---|---|---|---|---|---|
| 1 | 5 Dec | Albatros C | Spa73 | Langmarck |  | 5.387 | 5/12 |
|  | 1918 |  |  |  |  |  |  |
| 2 | 12 Apr | Halberstadt C | 103 | Corbeny | 1130 | 4.062 | 3/5 |
| – | 15 May | Two-seater (u/c) | 103 |  | 0945 | citation |  |
| 3(a) | 1 Aug | Albatros DIII | 13 | Vieville-en-Haye | 1850 | 10.065 | 6/8 |
| 4(a) | 1 Aug | Albatros DIII | 13 | Vieville-en-Haye | 1852 | 10.065 | 6/8 |
| 5 | 16 Aug | Rumpler C | 13 | Bouxieres | 0540 | 8.456 | 6/8 |
| 6(b) | 26 Sep | Fokker DVII | 13 | Flabes | 0735 | GO 11 |  |
| 7(c) | 18 Oct | Fokker DVII | 13 | Bantheville | 1410 | GO 21 |  |

(a) Shared with Lts H.B. Freeman, J.J. Seerley and W.H. Stovall; (b) Shared with Lts S.M. Avery and L. Brewer; (c) Shared with Lts S.M. Avery and W.H. Stovall.

## BISSELL Clayton Lawrence        Captain      148TH AERO

Born in Kane, Pennsylvania, 29 July 1896, 'Clay' received a law degree in 1917 from the Valpariso University, Indiana. He immediately joined the USAS and flew Sopwith Camels with the 148th Squadron, which was under RAF command in the summer and autumn of 1918. He received both the British DFC and American DSC, gaining six official victories. In 1919 he commanded the 639th Aero Squadron in the Army of Occupation in Germany. After the war he remained with the USAAC, rising to the rank of Major General. In the 1920's he was on the staff of General Billy Mitchell (1921-24) and led the flight which bombed and sank the *Ostrieland*, proving Mitchell's air power theories. On the night of the 3/4 August 1922, he made the first flight in darkness from Washington to New York. During WWII he served mainly in China, on General Joe Stillwell's staff and later commanded the US 10th Air Force in India. Later he became Chief of Intelligence. After WWII he was Air Attache in London between 1946-48, before retiring in 1950. He died on 24 September 1972, in Murfreesbro, Tennessee, aged 76.

### DFC CITATION

For skill and gallantry. On 28 October, this officer with his flight, attacked eight Fokker biplanes and after firing a short burst succeeded in shooting down one EA which crashed north of Jenlain. He was then attacked by three other Fokkers but outmanoeuvered them and finally shot down one which crashed close to the other. He finished this fight about 200 feet from the ground and was being severely machine-gunned by enemy infantry. This officer has served over four months with his squadron and has destroyed four EA and driven down three out of control. His courage, skill and disregard of danger have been worthy of the highest praise.

|  | 1918 |  |  |  |  |  |  |
|---|---|---|---|---|---|---|---|
| 1 | 21 Aug | Fokker DVII | 148 | Velu | 1940 | OOC | CR/ |
| 2 | 4 Sep | Fokker DVII | 148 | SW Marquin | 0710 | DES | CR/RAF |
| 3 | 4 Sep | Fokker DVII | 148 | W Marquin | 0715 | DES | CR/RAF |
| 4 | 3 Oct | Fokker DVII | 148 | Wambaix | 1107 | DES | CR/US |
| 5 | 28 Oct | Fokker DVII | 148 | NE Jenlain | 1205 | DES | CR/RAF |
| 6 | 28 Oct | Fokker DVII | 148 | NE Jenlain | 1208 | DES | CR/RAF |

## BISSONETTE Charles Arthur      Lieutenant    64 RAF, 24 RAF

From Los Angeles, California, he joined the RFC in March 1917, flying SE5As with 64 Squadron, from November 1917 to June 1918, claiming four victories. His 5th and 6th victories were two Albatros scouts which he caused to collide. After a period back in England, he joined 'B' Flight of 24 Squadron on 24 September, which also flew SE5s, but did not add to his score before the war ended, although he damaged and drove down one EA on 14 October. He remained with 24 until 3 February 1919.

| | 1918 | | | | | | |
|---|---|---|---|---|---|---|---|
| 1(a) | 17 Mar | Pfalz DIII | 64 | Biache | 1135 | OOC | CR/RAF |
| 2 | 23 Mar | Two-seater | 64 | Havrincourt Wood | 1110 | DES | CR/RAF |
| 3 | 9 May | Halberstadt C | 64 | Monchy | 1042 | OOC | CR/RAF |
| 4 | 9 May | Pfalz DIII | 64 | Boiry | 1043 | OOC | CR/RAF |
| 5 | 31 May | Albatros DV | 64 | La Bassee | 1940 | DES | CR/RAF |
| 6 | 31 May | Albatros DV | 64 | La Bassee | 1940 | DES | CR/RAF |

(a) Shared with Capt E.R. Tempest, Lts J.F.T. Barrett, Stringer and Hendrie.

## BOYSON Howard Koch     Lieutenant     66 RAF

From Dallas, Texas and Chicago, Illinois, Boyson was born in 1892. Volunteered for the RFC on 16 June 1917 while in Kirkland Lake, Canada when he was 26 and after pilot training went to No 66 Squadron which flew Sopwith Pups. When the Squadron went to Italy, flying Sopwith Camels, Boyson went with it. He received the Italian Silver Medal for Military Valor, surviving the war despite a bad crash in Camel B2472 while landing in fog on 29 January 1918.

| | 1917 | | | | | | |
|---|---|---|---|---|---|---|---|
| 1(a) | 8 Dec | Albatros DV | 66 | Valstagna | 1430 | OOC | ORB/SR |
| | 1918 | | | | | | |
| 2 | 3 May | Albatros DIII | 66 | Ormelle | 1145 | DES | ORB/SR/7 Bde |
| 3 | 10 May | Albatros DIII | 66 | Mount Meatta | 0930 | DES | ORB/SR/7 Bde |
| 4(b) | 26 May | LVG C | 66 | Salina | 0615 | DES | ORB/SR/7 Bde |
| 5(c) | 30 May | Albatros DIII | 66 | Moreno | 1555 | DES | ORB/SR/7 Bde |

(a) Believed to be Ltn Bertelsmeier of Jasta 39, who was captured; (b) Shared with Lt C. McEvoy; (c) OffStelv Karl Gebhard of Flik 41J, flying 153:219.

## BROOKS Arthur Raymond     Captain     139TH AND 22ND AERO

Born Framingham, Massachusetts on 1 November 1895, he attended the local school then graduated from MIT in 1917. Enlisted in the USAS at MIT in September 1917, going to Fort Wood, New York. Trained with the British RFC in Toronto, Canada, then to Hicks Field, Fort Worth, Texas with the 28th and 139th Squadrons for further training. Commissioned in February, 1918, he sailed for Europe in March, completing his training at Issoudun, France. Assigned to the 139th Aero he gained one victory before going to the 22nd Pursuit as a flight commander on 16 August. At the war's end he had added five more victories to his score (with four more unconfirmed) and won the DSC, having in fact been recommended for the Medal of Honor. After the Armistice he took command of the Squadron, being appointed Captain in March 1919. On his return from France he was stationed at both Selfridge and Kelly Fields, remaining with the Air Service until December 1922. Served again in WWII but spinal operations ended any hope of flying again for his country. He became Publications Manager with the Bell Telephone Company laboratories at Whippeny, New Jersey, and was a well known and respected WWI aviator in historical circles. His wife Ruth died in 1967. Always known as Ray he died in Summit, New Jersey, on 17 July 1991. As far as is known, he was the last surviving American air ace of WWI. Also received the Silver Star and the Aero Club of America's Medal of Merit.

### DSC CITATION

For extraordinary heroism in action over Mars-la-Tour, France, 14 September 1918. Lt Brooks, when his patrol was attacked by twelve enemy Fokkers, eight miles within the enemy lines, alone fought bravely and relentlessly with eight of them, pursuing the fight from 5,000 meters to within a few meters of the ground, and though his right rudder control was out and his plane riddled with bullets, he destroyed two Fokkers, one falling out of control, and the other bursting into flames.

| | 1918 | | | | | | |
|---|---|---|---|---|---|---|---|
| 1 | 29 Jul | Pfalz DIII | 139 | Heudicourt | | 5.172 | 3/8 |
| 2 | 2 Sep | Rumpler C | 22 | Armaucourt | 0930 | | |
| 3(a) | 4 Sep | Fokker DVII | 22 | Barnecourt | 1330 | GO5 | |
| 4(b) | 14 Sep | Fokker DVII | 22 | Mars-la-Tour | 1520 | GO7 | |
| 5(b) | 14 Sep | Fokker DVII | 22 | Mars-la-Tour | 1525 | GO7 | |
| 6(c) | 9 Oct | DFW C | 22 | Aincreville | 1435 | GO22 | |

(a) Shared with Lts C. Jones and F.B. Tyndall; (b) Shared with Lt P.E. Hassinger; (c) Shared with Lts J.D. Beane and C. Jones.

## BROWN Sydney MacGillvary        Lieutenant    29 RAF

Born Brooklyn, New York, 10 August 1895, he attended Princeton University until he joined the Royal Flying Corps in July 1917. Following pilot training in Canada and England, he was sent to 29 Squadron in France, flying SE5A scouts, posted on an auspicious day for an American – 4th July! By the end of the war he had destroyed four aircraft and a balloon to win the British DFC. This was Gazetted on 8 February 1919.

### DFC CITATION

On 28 October, when on offensive patrol, this officer, in company with three other machines, attacked nine Fokkers; three of the latter were destroyed, Second Lieutenant Brown accounting for one. In addition, he has three hostile aircraft and one balloon to his credit. He is a fearless and intrepid officer.

Brown went on leave on 3 November and was in England when the war ended. He returned to 29, stationed at Bickendorf, Germany, remaining there until mid-1919.

|   | 1918 |            |    |                  |      |     |        |
|---|------|------------|----|------------------|------|-----|--------|
| 1 | 12 Aug | Fokker DVII | 29 | S E Bailleul     | 1940 | DES | CR/RAF |
| 2 | 19 Aug | DFW C       | 29 | Bailleul-Nieppe Rd | 1120 | DES | CR/RAF |
| 3 | 29 Sep | Fokker DVII | 29 | Menin            | 1625 | DES | CR/RAF |
| 4 | 27 Oct | Balloon     | 29 | E Tournai        | 0920 | DES | CR/RAF |
| 5 | 28 Oct | Fokker DVII | 29 | S W Avelghem     | 1600 | DES | CR/RAF |

## BUCHANAN Archibald        Lieutenant    210 RAF

'Archie' was born on Long Island, New York on 5 October 1892. Sailed to England to join the Royal Naval Air Service but this became the RAF on 1 April 1918, when it merged with the RFC. Thus, after training he was posted to No 210 Squadron on 11 June 1918, formerly 10 Naval Squadron. Operating along the Flanders coast with the Sea Patrol and over Belgium, he accounted for six enemy aircraft and a balloon, receiving the DFC, which appeared in the London Gazette on 3 December. He landed at Ostend on 17 October, being informed by the local inhabitants that he was the first Allied combatant to enter the town since the Germans had left that morning. Not quite two weeks later, on 30 October, he was shot down in a fight with Fokker biplanes, spending the last twelve days of the war as a prisoner.

### DFC CITATION

On 29 September, this officer displayed great gallantry in an engagement with fifteen Fokker biplanes. Owing to engine trouble he was compelled to remain under his flight; he nevertheless accounted for two enemy machines, attacking one under its tail causing it to crash, and driving another down out of control. In addition to the foregoing, this officer has destroyed three machines and driven down two out of control.

|       | 1918 |            |     |                 |      |     |         |
|-------|------|------------|-----|-----------------|------|-----|---------|
| 1     | 30 Jun | Balloon     | 210 | N E Estaires    | 1110 | DES | CR/RAF  |
| 2 (a) | 20 Jul | Fokker DVII | 210 | S E Ostend      | 0945 | OOC | CR/5Gp  |
| 3     | 31 Jul | Fokker DVII | 210 | N W Wervicq     | 1830 | DES | CR/5Gp  |
| 4     | 11 Aug | Pfalz DIII  | 210 | S Westende      | 1050 | OOC | CR/5Gp  |
| 5     | 16 Sep | Fokker DVII | 210 | N Zeebrugge     | 1115 | DES | CR/5Gp  |
| 6     | 29 Sep | Fokker DVII | 210 | Wijnendaele Wood | 0800 | DES | CR/5Gp  |
| 7     | 29 Sep | Fokker DVII | 210 | Wijnendaele Wood | 0805 | OOC | CR/5Gp  |

(a) Shared with Captain H.T. Mellings.

## BUCKLEY Harold Robert        Captain    95TH AERO

From Westfield, Massachusetts, where he was born 4 April 1896. Educated at the Phillips Andover Academy and excelled at sport. Entered the American Ambulance Service in March 1917, serving in France for four months before enlisting in the US Air Service in Paris in August. Trained at Tours, Issoudun and Cazaux, then received an assignment to join the 95th Pursuit in March 1918. He saw active service in the Champagne Sector, then Toul in May and June, the Chateau Thierry drive in July and August and then the Argonne offensive in the last months of the war. He had been commissioned in December 1917 and promoted to Captain on 1 November 1918. He received the DSC and Oak Leaf, the French Croix de Guerre and the Medal of the Aero Club of America. After the war he lived in Paris for some years and in 1933 wrote a history of his old 95th Aero — *Squadron 95* — which was illustrated with drawings by Lansing Holden, another ace of the 95th. Buckley died in Rigby, Idaho, on 13 June 1958.

He was mentioned in a General Order (No 12.058 'D' GHQ) French Armies of the East, on 29 November 1918; "A calm and determined pursuit pilot and patrol leader. Has attacked planes and balloons and fired at troops on the ground from low altitude. On 30 May 1918, together with his patrol, he attacked two enemy planes, one of which he brought down, the other being driven down in a damaged condition."

### DSC CITATION

For extraordinary heroism in action near Perles, France, 10 August 1918. Lt Buckley was on a patrol protecting a French bi-place observation machine when they were suddenly set upon by six enemy planes. Lt Buckley attacked and destroyed the nearest and the remainder fled into their own territory. He then carried on with his mission until he had escorted the Allied plane safely to its own aerodrome.

### OAK LEAF CLUSTER CITATION

For extraordinary heroism in action near Reville, France, 26-27 September 1918. Lt Buckley dived through a violent and heavy anti-aircraft and machine-gun fire and set on fire an enemy balloon that was being lowered into its nest. The next day while leading a patrol he met and sent down in flames an enemy plane while it was engaged in reglage work.

|      | 1918   |             |    |                  |      |        |      |
|------|--------|-------------|----|------------------|------|--------|------|
| 1(a) | 30 May | Two-seater  | 95 | Apremont-Jaulny  | 0800 | 2291   | VIII |
| 2    | 10 Aug | Fokker DVII | 95 | Perles           |      | 17.079 | 10/8 |
| 3(b) | 26 Sep | Balloon     | 95 | Reville          | 0605 | GO5    |      |
| 4(c) | 27 Sep | Rumpler C   | 95 | Montfaucon       | 1814 | GO12   |      |
| 5(c) | 27 Sep | Rumpler C   | 95 | Fleville         | 1925 | GO17   |      |

(a) Shared with Lts W.V. Casgrain, J.A. Hambleton, S.E. McKeown and J.L. Mitchell; (b) Shared with Lt A.H. McLanahan; (c) Shared with Lts T.F. Butz, E.P. Curtis, H.J. Popperfuss and G.O. Woodward.

## BURDICK Howard          Lieutenant          17TH AERO

From Brooklyn, New York, he became a member of the 17th Aero Squadron under the command of the RAF in 1918, flying Sopwith Camels. He was awarded the DFC for his eight victories, often flying in company with George Vaughn his flight commander. The Fokker biplane they shot down on 14 October, force landed and the pilot was killed when shot up on the ground. During the Second World War his son Clinton D. Burdick followed in his father's footsteps, flying P51 Mustangs with the US 356th Fighter Group of the 8th Air Force in England, destroying 5.5 Lufwaffe aircraft to become an ace like his father.

### DFC CITATION

For skill and gallantry. On 25 October, while on an offensive patrol, this officer attacked a formation of five Fokker biplanes over the forest of Mormal and succeeded in shooting down one in flames. On another occasion he dived on an enemy two-seater but was in turn attacked by two Fokkers, one of which he succeeded in shooting down in flames. Later he attacked three enemy aircraft who were attacking one of our machines and shot down one which dived straight into the ground and crashed. This officer has now destroyed five EA (three in flames) and has at all times displayed the greatest gallantry, skill and disregard of danger.

|      | 1918   |                |    |                 |      |     |        |
|------|--------|----------------|----|-----------------|------|-----|--------|
| 1    | 18 Sep | LVG C          | 17 | Rumilly         | 1100 | DES | CR/RAF |
| 2    | 24 Sep | Fokker DVII    | 17 | N W Havrincourt | 1040 | DES | CR/RAF |
| 3    | 28 Sep | LVG C          | 17 |                 | 1745 | DES | CR/RAF |
| 4    | 28 Sep | Fokker DVII    | 17 | Cambrai         | 1810 | DES | CR/RAF |
| 5(a) | 2 Oct  | DFW C          | 17 | E Awoignt       | 0910 | DES | CR/RAF |
| 6(b) | 14 Oct | Halberstadt C  | 17 | E Bazeul        | 0710 | DES | CR/RAF |
| 7(a) | 14 Oct | Fokker DVII    | 17 | N E Hausey      | 1400 | DES | CR/US  |
| 8    | 25 Oct | Fokker DVII    | 17 | Mormal Woods    | 1055 | DES | CR/RAF |

(a) Shared with Lt G.A. Vaughn; (b) Shared with Lt G.A. Vaughn and Lt L. Myers.

## CALLAHAN Lawrence Kingsley          Lieutenant          85 RAF, 148TH AERO

Born Louisville, Kentucky, 11 January 1894, he was a graduate of Cornell College and resided in Chicago, Illinois. He joined the USAS and was sent to England for advanced flight training with the Royal Flying Corps. He was well known through the writings of fellow pilot Elliott W. Springs, especially in the book *War Birds: the diary of an unknown aviator*. Larry Callahan and Springs both went to 85 Squadron in France in April 1918, flying SE5As with Larry gaining three victories. He then joined the 148th, having to switch to flying Sopwith Camels, added two more victories and received the British DFC in December. He served with the 148th from 24 August till the war's end. During WWII he served in the USAAC, part of his duty taking him to the 12th US Air Force in Oran, in Algeria. He died on 17 September 1977, in Gardena, California, aged 83.

### DFC CITATION

For gallantry and skill. On 28 October, this officer, whilst leading his flight, attacked a formation of seven Fokkers and after firing a short burst at one EA, sent it down completely out of control N W of Jenlain, and drove another EA off the tail of one of his flight. His flight in this fight accounted for six EA crashed and one out of control without losing a machine, a result largely due to his skilful leading. On another occasion he engaged a formation of EA over Esnes and succeeded in shooting down one of the EA which crashed near Esnes. This officer has accounted for four EA crashed and one driven down out of control; he has proven himself an exceptionally fine patrol leader and has at all times displayed gallantry, initiative and devotion to duty of the highest order.

|   | 1918 |  |  |  |  |  |  |
|---|---|---|---|---|---|---|---|
| 1 | 16 Jun | Two-seater | 85 | Estaires | 0720 | DES | CR/RAF |
| 2 | 13 Jul | Fokker DVII | 85 | Armentieres | 2030 | DES | CR/RAF |
| 3 | 24 Jul | Fokker DVII | 85 | Neuve Eglise | 1040 | OOC | CR/ |
| 4 | 3 Oct | Fokker DVII | 148 | Esnes | 1110 | DES | CR/RAF |
| 5 | 28 Oct | Fokker DVII | 148 | N W Jenlain | 1205 | DES | CR/US |

## CALLENDER Alvin Andrew      Captain      32 RAF

Born in New Orleans, Independence Day, 4 July 1893. He joined the RFC at Camp Borden, Canada in June 1917. Trained in Fort Worth, Texas and England, where he was at the Central Flying School, then sent to 32 Squadron, flying SE5As, on 15 May 1918. Not long after he had scored his second victory he was himself shot down, on 10 June, but survived unhurt. He became a flight commander in early September but on 30 October he was shot down again, in SE5 No E6010. It is believed his victor was Oberleutnant von Griesheim of Jasta Boelcke, the German's only confirmed victory. He fell within the British lines but died of his wounds. A fine collection of his letters and photographs was published privately by his family in 1978, entitled *War in an Open Cockpit*.

|   | 1918 |  |  |  |  |  |  |
|---|---|---|---|---|---|---|---|
| 1 | 28 May | Pfalz DIII | 32 | Armentieres | 1830 | OOC | CR/ORB/SR |
| 2 | 6 Jun | Fokker DVII | 32 | Montdidier | 1900 | OOC | CR/ORB/SR |
| 3 | 8 Jul | Fokker DVII | 32 | Bauvin | 0810 | OOC | CR/ORB/SR |
| 4 | 25 Jul | Fokker DVII | 32 | Fismes | 1930 | DES | CR/RAF |
| 5 | 10 Aug | Fokker DVII | 32 | Peronne | 1140 | OOC | CR/ORB/SR |
| 6 | 16 Sep | Fokker DVII | 32 | Sancourt | 1810 | OOC | CR/ORB/SR |
| 7 | 24 Sep | Fokker DVII | 32 | N Bourlon Wood | 1705 | OOC | CR/ORB/SR |
| 8 | 24 Sep | Fokker DVII | 32 | N Bourlon Wood | 1710 | OOC | CR/ORB/SR |

## CAMPBELL Douglas      Lieutenant      94TH AERO

From St Jose, near San Francisco, California, born 7 June 1896, he attended Harvard University and then lived in Mt Hamilton. While at Cornell University he began ground school training in aviation, and went overseas in August 1917 to complete his training at Issoudon. Assigned to the 94th Pursuit Squadron on 1 March 1918, he and Alan Winslow were credited with the first two victories of the Squadron on 14 April, which were also the first victories recorded by American trained pilots of the USAS. Doug Campbell went on to claim six victories before he was wounded on 5th June, continuing the air battle despite a bullet in the back. He received the DSC with four Oak Leaf Clusters, the French Legion d'Honneur and Croix de Guerre with two palms. He went back to the USA, returning to France to rejoin the 94th shortly after the Armistice. In 1935 he was with Pan American Airways, with whom he became Vice President in 1939 and General Manager in 1948. In all he was with PanAm for 24 years until he retired to Cos Cob, Connecticut, in 1963. He and his wife had four sons and two daughters, and he died in Greenwich, Conn, on 16 December 1990, at the age of 94.

### DSC (FIRST) CITATION

For extraordinary heroism in action on 19 May 1918. Lt Campbell attacked an enemy biplace at an altitude of 4,500 meters east of Flirey, France. He rushed in to attack but after shooting a few rounds his gun jammed. Undeterred by this accident, he manoeuvred so as to protect himself, corrected the jam in mid-air and returned to the assault. After a short and violent action, the enemy plane took fire and crashed to the earth.

His three Oak Leaf citations were for actions on 27 May, 28 May, 31 May and 5 June 1918. His Croix de Guerre was in recognition of his first victory on 14 April, when he shot down Vzfw Wronicki (PoW) of Jasta 64.

| | 1918 | | | | | | |
|---|---|---|---|---|---|---|---|
| 1 | 14 Apr | Pfalz DIII | 94 | Gengault, Toul | 0853 | 15.420 | 14/4 |
| 2 | 18 May | Rumpler C | 94 | Bonzee-en-Woevre | 1135 | 25.662 | 19/5 |
| 3 | 19 May | Rumpler C | 94 | E of Flirey | 1135 | 25.662 | 19/5 |
| 4 | 27 May | Pfalz DIII | 94 | Montsec | 1006 | 35.372 | 27/5 |
| 5 | 31 May | Rumpler C | 94 | Lironville | 0805 | 3 | 31/5 |
| 6(a) | 5 Jun | Rumpler C | 94 | Mailly | 1020 | US/133 | |

(a) Shared with Lt J.A. Meissner.
All Campbell's victories have been identified; (1) Jasta 64; (2) FA(A)279; (3) FA(A)298b; (4) Jasta 65; (5) FA(A)242; (6) FA12.

## CASSADY Thomas Gantz      Captain      SPA157, SPA163, 28TH AERO

From Spencer, Indiana, he was born 5 January 1896 at Waterloo, Iowa. Graduated from the University of Chicago in 1914 and joined the US Ambulance Service, then the French Foreign Legion in order to transfer to French Aviation in July 1917. Assigned to Spa157 on 26 December 1917 as a Sergeant, until he transferred to the USAS in February 1918 and commissioned. Served with the 103rd Aero but was then assigned to Spa163 from 14 May to 8 September 1918, on which date he went to the 28th Pursuit as a flight commander where he remained till the end of the war. He made Captain in March 1919. He was awarded the DSC and Oak Leaf, the French Legion d'Honneur and Croix de Guerre with three palms and one star. He scored five victories with the French and four more with the USAS. After the war he went into the investment business in Chicago. During WWII he worked with the French underground, going to Vichy France as Naval attache but really assigned with the OSS to aid the escape lines. In civilian clothes he made four spy trips into occupied France. When the Germans occupied Vichy in November 1942, he was arrested and detained until February 1944. Returning to under-cover work in Algiers for the OSS he helped in the pre-invasion planning of Southern France. Following the liberation of Paris he was put in charge of all intelligence personnel there. He died from cancer, in Lake Forest, Illinois on 9 July 1972, aged 76.

### DSC CITATION

For extraordinary heroism in action near Fismes, 28 May 1918 and near Epieds, France, 5 June 1918. On 28 May, Lt Cassady, single-handed, attacked an LVG German plane which crashed near Fismes. On 5 June, as patrol leader of five Spads, while being attacked by twelve German Fokkers (sic), he brought down one of the enemy planes near Epieds and by his dash and courage, broke the enemy formation.

### OAK LEAF CITATION

For the following act of heroism: on 15 August 1918, near Saint-Marie, while acting as protection for a Salmson, he was attacked by seven Fokkers, two of which he brought down and enabled the Salmson to accomplish its mission and return safely.

### LEGION D'HONNEUR CITATION

Came to serve France at a time when there was no military obligation or compulsion. Object of a brilliant citation and gravely wounded in the Medical Section. Has since passed to aviation where he is indispensible in turn by the greatness of his character, his skill as a pilot, and his absolute disregard for danger. Officially credited with five enemy planes.

Cassidy was also cited in orders on 5 June (twice), 12 July, 20 August, and 30 October 1918.

| | 1918 | | | | | | |
|---|---|---|---|---|---|---|---|
| 1(a) | 28 May | LVG C | Spa163 | Savigny | 1330 | 38.882 | 30/5 |
| 2 | 5 Jun | Albatros DV | Spa163 | Epieds | | 22.586 | 18/6 |
| 3(b) | 23 Jun | Halberstadt CLII | Spa163 | Ferte Gaucher | | 29.237 | 23/6 |
| – | 29 Jul | Two-seater | Spa163 | Cornilette | 1745 | 192* | 29/7 |
| –(c) | 1 Aug | Two-seater | Spa163 | Montspar | 1150 | 199* | 1/8 |
| 4(d) | 11 Aug | Two-seater | Spa163 | Betheniville | 1205 | 18.893 | 11/8 |
| 5(e) | 15 Aug | Fokker DVII | Spa163 | St Marie-a-Py | | 230* | 15/8 |
| –(e) | 15 Aug | Fokker DVII | Spa163 | St Marie-a-Py | | 230* | 15/8 |
| 6(f) | 14 Sep | Fokker DVII | 28 | Villers-sur-Troy | 0733 | GO 11 | |
| 7 | 26 Sep | Fokker DVII | 28 | St Marie-a-Py | 0723 | GO 17 | |
| 8(g) | 2 Oct | Halberstadt C | 28 | Iviory | 1750 | GO17 | |
| 9(h) | 27 Oct | Two-seater | 28 | Briquesny | 1500 | GO 23 | |

(a) Shared with Lt W.T. Ponder and Caporal Dequeker; (b) Shared with Sergents M. Guillet and S Lederlin; aircraft from

Schutzstaffel 26 force landed inside French lines and the crew were captured; (c) Shared with Sergents J.A. Connelly and A.A. Cook; (d) Shared with Lt W.T. Ponder and Sergent A.A. Cook (US); (e) Shared with Sergents J.A. Connelly and Penevynck; (second Fokker apparently not officially confirmed). (f) Shared with Lts H.C. Allen, E.J. Hardy, W.T. Jebb, C.I. Merrick and L.P. Moriarty; (g) Shared with Lts J.R. Hardendorf, E.J. Hardy, W.T. Jebb, J.F. Merrill, A.H. Smith and M. Stenseth; (h) Shared with Lts B.E. Brown and G.W. Furlow.
(*)Confirmed in IVe Armee Reports, and/or citations.

## CATTO Charles Gray       Lieutenant      45 RAF

Born Dallas, Texas, on 7 November 1896, he went to Britain to become a medical student and was studying at Edinburgh University, Scotland, when the war began. Although he tried to enlist, his parents refused permission. They then told him he could only continue his studies if he promised not to join the army. He agreed, and later, in June 1917, joined instead, the Royal Flying Corps! He completed his flight training then left for Italy to join 45 Squadron, flying Camels, in March 1918. He claimed six enemy machines, one of which fell inside Allied lines — a Brandenburg C-type of Flik 8D, piloted by Flugsfuhrer Alois Gnamusch and Leutnant Rudolf Huss. He also served with the Squadron when it returned to the Western Front in late 1918. Catto returned to complete his studies in Edinburgh, returning to the USA to become a doctor in his native Texas. He died on 24 June 1972.

|       | 1918   |               |    |                   |      |      |         |
|-------|--------|---------------|----|-------------------|------|------|---------|
| 1(a)  | 19 May | Aviatik C     | 45 | Mel               | 0625 | DES  | CR/14W  |
| 2(b)  | 22 May | Two-seater    | 45 | Levada            | 0920 | DES  | CR/14W  |
| 3     | 7 Jun  | Brandenburg C | 45 | Cismon            | 0935 | CAPT | CR/14W  |
| 4     | 15 Jun | Aviatik C     | 45 | Mt Campo-Poselaro | 0745 | OOC  | CR/14W  |
| 5     | 20 Jun | Albatros DIII | 45 | Nerversa          | 1040 | OOC  | ORB/14W |
| 6     | 5 Aug  | Scout         | 45 | Mt Grappa         | 1030 | DES  | ORB/14W |

(a) Shared with Capt N.C. Jones; (b) Shared with Capt G. Bush.

## CHAMBERS Reed McKinley      Major      94TH AERO

From Memphis, Tennessee, born 18 August 1894, in Onaga, Kansas. He joined the Tennessee National Guard in 1914, serving on the Mexican border in 1916. Transferred to the USAS and after flight training was assigned to the 94th Pursuit Squadron. He was credited with 7 official victories, won the DSC with 3 Oak Leaves, the French Legion d'Honneur (citation dated 29 November 1918) and Croix de Guerre with two palms, one silver star and one bronze star. Post war he flew as a test pilot, then in 1925 headed Florida Airways with wartime friend Eddie Rickenbacker, but due to loss of airplanes in a crash and a hurricane, the company was forced into bankrupcy in 1927. Learning from this experience, he then formed an American Insurance Group to cover aviation insurance. In 1968 he flew in a two-seater F106 jet, taking over the controls long enough to go through the sound barrier. He died 16 January 1972, aged 77, at St Thomas in the Virgin Islands.

### DSC CITATION

For extraordinary heroism in action over the region of Epinonville, France, 29 September 1918. While on a mission, Lt Chambers, accompanied by another machine piloted by Lt Samuel Kaye Jr, encountered a formation of six enemy machines (Fokker type) at an altitude of 3,000 feet. Despite numerical superiority of the enemy, Lt Chambers and Lt Kaye immediately attacked and succeeded in destroying one and forced the remaining five to retreat to their own lines.

His three Oak Leaf Clusters were awarded for actions on 2 October (two) and 22 October.

### LEGION D'HONNEUR CITATION

A very brave pilot, who, by dint of his sterling qualities was a fine example for the whole squadron. While he was on patrol with eight of his comrades, he attacked 24 enemies who were scattered and he came back in our lines with his plane severely damaged.

|      | 1918   |                |    |            |      |       |
|------|--------|----------------|----|------------|------|-------|
| 1    | 26 Sep | Balloon        | 94 | Nantillois | 0552 | GO 17 |
| 2(a) | 29 Sep | Fokker DVII    | 94 | Cunel      | 1720 | GO 13 |
| 3(b) | 2 Oct  | Hannover CL (*) | 94 | Montfaucon | 1730 | GO 14 |
| 4    | 2 Oct  | Fokker DVII    | 94 | Vilosnes   | 1740 | GO 14 |
| 5    | 10 Oct | Fokker DVII    | 94 | Doulcon    | 1548 | GO 20 |
| 6    | 22 Oct | Fokker DVII    | 94 | Vilosnes   | 1630 | GO 22 |
| 7    | 22 Oct | Fokker DVII    | 94 | Vilosnes   | 1632 | GO 22 |

(a) Shared with Lt S. Kaye Jr; (b) Shared with Lt E.V. Rickenbacker. (*) This victory is often listed as being a Halberstadt two-seater, but Chambers confirmed to the authors it was in fact a Hannover.

# CLAY Jr Henry Robinson    Lieutenant    43 RAF, 148TH AERO

Born Plattsburg, Missouri, 27 November 1895, he later lived in Fort Worth Texas. 'Hank' Clay was a member of the first detachment of US aviation cadets to be sent to Oxford, England, for advanced flight training. He was then posted to 43 Squadron in France, flying Camels, for operational experience and on 30 May 1918, shot down an enemy aircraft but it was not confirmed. He was then assigned to the 148th on 2 July, became the 'C' Flight Commander, receiving both the British DFC and American DSC. Towards the end of the war he was put in command of the 41st Aero but the war ended before it could get to the front. Clay died in the great influenza epidemic, in Coblenz, Germany, 17 February 1919. His father received his son's posthumous DSC at Fort Worth in 1920.

### DFC CITATION

On 16 August, while leading his patrol, they were attacked by six Fokker biplanes over Noyon. Lt Clay shot down one in flames and with his flight drove the others east. On 27 August, with another of his flight, he attacked a two-seater over Remy. After a short burst the wing came off and the EA was seen to crash by three other pilots. On 4 September, while two flights of his squadron, led by Lt Clay, were patrolling with two flights of No 60 Squadron, RAF, they were engaged by ten Fokker biplanes. In the fight which ensued, he shot an EA off the tail of an SE5. It was seen to crash and burn up on the ground by a pilot of No 60 Squadron. A moment later Lt Clay attacked two EA on the tail of one of his patrol, one of which was seen to crash. This fight started at 4,000 feet and ended at 800 feet. Lt Clay's flight accounted for three EA crashed and one out of control. This officer has been on active service since 17 March 1918. He has destroyed five EA (one two-seater shared with Lt T.L. Moore) and driven down out of control one. He has exhibited on all occasions, admirable qualities of leadership and has moulded his flight into a most effective fighting unit.

### DSC CITATION

For extraordinary heroism in action near Sains-les-Marquins, France, 4 September 1918. In an action wherein Lt Clay's patrol was outnumbered two to one, he attacked the group and shot down the enemy aircraft in flames. He continued in the combat and later attacked two enemy aircraft which were pursuing a plane of his patrol and succeeded in shooting one enemy aircraft down. Again on 27 September1918, near Cambrai, with one other pilot, Lt Clay observed five enemy planes approaching our lines and although hopelessly outnumbered, immediately attacked and singled out a plane which was seen to crash to the ground. He was immediately attacked by the other enemy planes and compelled to fight his way back to our base.

|  | 1918 |  |  |  |  |  |  |
|---|---|---|---|---|---|---|---|
| 1 | 16 Aug | Fokker DVII | 148 | N Noyon | 1555 | DES | CR/RAF |
| 2 | 21 Aug | Fokker DVII | 148 | Velu-Beaumetz | 1940 | OOC | CR/ |
| 3 | 25 Aug | Fokker DVII | 148 | N Bapaume | 1856 | DES | CR/RAF |
| 4(a) | 27 Aug | DFW C | 148 | Remy | 1305 | DES | CR/RAF |
| 5 | 4 Sep | Fokker DVII | 148 | Marquion | 0710 | DES | CR/RAF |
| 6 | 4 Sep | Fokker DVII | 148 | Marquion | 0714 | DES | CR/RAF |
| 7 | 24 Sep | Fokker DVII | 148 | Bourlon | 0735 | DES | CR/US |
| 8(b) | 27 Sep | Halberstadt C | 148 | Fontaine | 0955 | DES | CR/RAF |

(a) Shared with Lt T.L. Moore; (b) Shared with Lt E.W. Springs.

# COLER Eugene Seeley    Lieutenant    11 RAF

From Newark, New Jersey, born 13 January 1896, he joined up in Canada and by 1918 was a two-seater Bristol Fighter pilot with No 11 Squadron. He and his gunners claimed 16 victories and he received the British DFC, Gazetted 3 December 1918, before being wounded on 16 September, in a fight with Jasta Boelcke. After the war he returned to university studies, became a doctor and set up a practice in New York. In 1942 he joined the USAAC as a Major, serving with the 319th Bomb Group in North Africa and later with the 8th Air Force in England. He was called up again in 1951, becoming Divisional Air Surgeon in England at HQ, 7th Air Division, until he died on 30 August 1953, at Gerrard's Cross, Buckinghamshire. He held the rank of Colonel. He had received the Legion of Merit, Air Medal and Bronze Star. One unique feature of his combat career — he never claimed less than two victories in a single fight!

### DFC CITATION

Bold in attack and skilful in manoeuvre, this officer never hesitates to engage the enemy, regardless of disparity in numbers. On 13 August when on escort duty, he dived on a formation of twenty enemy aeroplanes. In the engagement that ensued he himself destroyed three and his observer two — making a total of five machines destroyed in the fight; a fine performance, reflecting great credit on the officers concerned.

| | 1918 | | | | | | |
|---|---|---|---|---|---|---|---|
| 1(a) | 9 May | Pfalz DIII | 11 | Albert-Combles | 1220 | OOC | CR/RAF |
| 2(a) | 9 May | Pfalz DIII | 11 | Albert-Combles | 1220 | OOC | CR/RAF |
| 3(a) | 9 May | Pfalz DIII | 11 | Albert-Combles | 1220 | OOC | CR/RAF |
| 4(a) | 13 Aug | Fokker DVII | 11 | Peronne | 0840 | DES | CR/RAF |
| 5(a) | 13 Aug | Fokker DVII | 11 | Peronne | 0840 | OOC | CR/RAF |
| 6(a) | 13 Aug | Fokker DVII | 11 | Peronne | 0841 | OOC | CR/RAF |
| 7(a) | 13 Aug | Fokker DVII | 11 | Peronne | 0842 | DES | CR/RAF |
| 8(a) | 13 Aug | Fokker DVII | 11 | Peronne | 0842 | DES | CR/RAF |
| 9(b) | 30 Aug | Fokker DVII | 11 | N W Havrincourt | 1840 | DES | CR/ |
| 10(b) | 30 Aug | Pfalz DXII | 11 | N W Havrincourt | 1840 | DES | CR/ |
| 11(c) | 6 Sep | Fokker DVII | 11 | W Cambrai | 1030 | DES | CR/RAF |
| 12(c) | 6 Sep | Fokker DVII | 11 | W Cambrai | 1030 | DES | CR/RAF |
| 13(d) | 15 Sep | Fokker DVII | 11 | W Esnes | 1200 | DES | CR/RAF |
| 14(d) | 15 Sep | Fokker DVII | 11 | E Esnes | 1200 | DES | CR/RAF |
| 15(d) | 16 Sep | Pfalz DXII | 11 | E Cambrai | 0830 | DES | CR/RAF |
| 16(d) | 16 Sep | Fokker DVII | 11 | E Cambrai | 0830 | DES | CR/RAF |

(a) Observers; Lt C.W. Gladman; (b) Lt B.E.J.D. Tuke; (c) D.P. Conyngham; (d) Lt E.J. Corbett.

## CONNELLY Jr James Alexander    Adjutant    SPA157, SPA163

From Philadephia, Pennsylvania, Connelly joined the 1st Regiment of the French Foreign Legion, transferred to the Aviation Service within the aegis of the Lafayette Flying Corps and gained his Military Flying Brevet, No 9711, on 3 November 1917. Assigned to Spa157 on 15 January 1918, he gained two victories before going to Spa163 on 27 June. With this unit he scored five more victories between 27 June and the end of the war. From the French he received the Medaille Militaire and Croix de Guerre (cited in orders on 16 August, 22 August and in November 1918), and from his own country the DSC. He died in New York on 2 February 1944.

### MEDAILLE MILITAIRE CITATION

Voluntarily enlisted for the duration of the war, has become indispensable by greatness of his character, his qualities as a pilot, and his complete contempt for danger. On 6 September 1918, he reported his fifth victory by downing an enemy scout. Three citations.

### DSC CITATION

Distinguished himself by extraordinary heroism in connection with military operations against an armed enemy of the United States at Suippes, France, on 6 September 1918, and in recognition of his gallant conduct, I have awarded him, in the name of the President, the Distinguished Service Cross. Signed, J.J. Pershing, Commander-in-Chief, USAS.

| | 1918 | | | | | | |
|---|---|---|---|---|---|---|---|
| 1(a) | 20 Apr | Balloon | Spa157 | Selles | | 22.352 | 20/4 |
| 2(b) | 5 Jun | EA | Spa157 | | | 7.087 | 6/6 |
| –(c) | 1 Aug | Two-seater | Spa163 | Montspar | 1150 | 199. | 1/8 |
| 3(d) | 13 Aug | Two-seater | Spa163 | St Martin l'Heureux | | 22.001 | 13/8 |
| 4(e) | 15 Aug | Fokker DVII | Spa163 | St Marie-a-Py | | IVe230 | 15/8 |
| –(e) | 15 Aug | Fokker DVII(u/c) | Spa163 | St Marie-a-Py | | IVe230 | 15/8 |
| 5(f) | 6 Sep | Fokker DVII | Spa163 | Naravin | 0830 | 8.456 | 6/9 |
| 6 | 28 Sep | Balloon | Spa163 | Challeronge | 1115 | 40.778 | 28/9 |
| 7 | 4 Nov | Fokker DVII | Spa163 | Suzanne | 1215 | 6.943 | 5/11 |

(a) Shared with Sergent Jacob; (b) Shared with Adjutant Viguier and Sergent Baugham; (c) Shared with Lt Cassady and Sgt A.A. Cook; (d) Shared with MdL E. Fery and Caporal R. Onillon; (e) Shared with Lt T.G. Cassady and Sergent Penevynck; (f) Shared with MdL J. Morvan.

## COOK Everett Richard    Captain    91ST AERO

Born Indianapolis, Indiana, 13 December 1894 but lived in Memphis, Tennessee as a child. Volunteered for the Air Service in May 1917 and by 1918 was in France. Took command of the 91st Observation Squadron on 6 September. For his war service he received the DSC, Legion d'Honneur, Croix de Guerre and palm. His observers claimed five victories in which he shared credit. Observer for his first victory was Lt W.R. Lawson, while Lt William Badham scored the other four. In the 1920's, Cook was on the staff of General Billy Mitchell and after leaving the service became a member of the Cotton Exchange in Memphis, and its President in 1931.